T0265838

"*The CFO in Pole Position* is a must-read for CFOs and their senior finance teams to understand the power of data and revolutionize decision-making. Many organizations focus too much on the technology and short-term decision-making. This book helps CFOs to take the lead in really transforming the company's decision-making process and focus on what is really important."

René Hooft Graafland, member of the supervisory board of Ahold Delhaize, Koninklijke FrieslandCampina N.V. and of Lucas Bols N.V., former CFO and member of the executive board of Heineken N.V.

"A highly recommended read for CFO's who want to lead their organization in taking the best decisions in these turbulent times. It's not a handbook, but it will definitely inspire finance leaders to go for pole position. The authors make it clear: it's not only about mastering the technology but, maybe more important, to master the data and act upon it."

Prof. dr. F.H.M. Verbeeten MBA, professor at Amsterdam Business School and vice Program director Executive Master Finance & Control program at the University of Amsterdam

Mohamed Bouker | Frank Geelen | Nart Wielaard

# THE CFO
# IN POLE
# POSITION

## LEADING NEXT-GENERATION DECISION-MAKING
## IN A DATA-DRIVEN ORGANIZATION

Boom | Management IMPACT

Jacket design: Paul Olsman, H2R+ Design, www.h2rplus.nl
Layout: Michel Wassenaar, Perfect Service, www.perfectservice.nl
Copy editing: Carrie Ballard, Atelier English, www.atelierenglish.com

© 2020 Mohamed Bouker, Frank Geelen, Nart Wielaard & Boom
uitgevers Amsterdam
Management Impact is a division of Boom uitgevers Amsterdam

ISBN 978 94 6276 390 6
e-ISBN 978 94 6276 391 3

# TABLE OF CONTENTS

# Introduction

Formula 1 racing is approaching a historic moment – machines are about to outperform even the best professional racing drivers.

Former world champion Sebastian Vettel was very clear about this. He argued that telemetry systems have been given a far too dominant role in motor sport. In the past, when a driver was the fastest at taking a chicane, it was because he was following his own course, and if he did this right, he would keep his lead for the whole racing weekend. Today, with abundant data, everything is so transparent and systemised that it is the engineers who suggest the even better course to follow. [1]

Compare that with a famous statement by another former champion, American Mario Andretti, who decades ago said, 'If you think you're in control, you're just not going fast enough'. At the time, this typified a racing world in which everything revolved around the driver and his unique qualities, which included a healthy dose of bravery and courage.

Within only a few decades, top class racing has turned itself upside down, and the exact reverse of Andretti's quote has in fact become true: 'If you're in control, you can go faster'.

This revolution is based on data – huge amounts of it. With this data, computer systems make instant decisions about tyre choice, the optimal line to follow on the circuit track, timing of pit stops, engine management as well as many other things. It enables drivers to be more in control so that they can go just that little bit faster.

Now that car performance is so similar among top teams – differences in lap times have become extremely small – it has become increasingly clear that he who makes the best decisions wins the race. And we simply have to acknowledge that computers are much better at this than any driver.

All of this is true in the corporate world as well.

In business, better information also leads to better decisions. In a data-driven era, successful competition increasingly revolves around this simple principle. And those unable to keep up will soon be out of business. In the not too distant future, almost every decision will be the result of data analysis, and the human factor will play either only a marginal role or an entirely different one.

Just as Sebastian Vettel is experiencing first-hand how such systems are impacting the racing profession, so too must top business managers take a step back and hand their decision-making autonomy over to computers.

Business leaders all agree that this is what they should do, but strangely enough hardly anyone behaves accordingly.

As far as information processing systems and technology are concerned, many organizations are still stuck in the proverbial Dark Ages. They have become addicted to a world of slow systems, are not able to change their firmly established routines, and have trouble understanding the vital importance of reliable information.

No business leader worth their salt should accept this type of inertia. Much is at stake. The challenge is to become a Decision Oriented Organization, an organization that excels in speed and quality of decisions based on data. Those who fail to transform their organization into this kind of well-oiled information processing machine will lose the battle in the corporate arena.

One may think that this line of reasoning is only valid in predictable circumstances and relatively calm markets.

This couldn't be further from the truth.

Excelling in decision-making is especially important in crisis situations and in highly ambiguous and chaotic dynamics. In the eye of a storm, organizations that are in control of their data and have sophisticated systems for scenario planning and exploring a wealth of internal and external data are best prepared. This has been demonstrated in numerous cases in which companies were in crisis. It was also demonstrated in the financial crisis that shook the world in 2008. And in the extreme turbulence following the outbreak of the COVID-19 virus, it once again became clear that the future of many organizations was largely determined by their ability to take smart and quick decisions based on reliable and relevant data.

These times of crisis underpin one simple truth we mentioned before:

The ones who are in control of their information can go faster. And will therefore be the winners.

All of this stresses the fact that organizations need to transform their decision-making processes. Chief Financial Officers (CFOs) are best equipped to manage this transformation into a Decision Oriented Organization. They understand the value of tracking and analyzing data.

Many CFOs have long since outgrown the antiquated role of bean counter and have become fully fledged sparring partners in practically all strategic areas. Now it is time for the next phase. We are convinced they can learn from Formula 1 teams how to build a Decision Oriented Organization. CFOs are the ones in pole position to help their organizations excel in data processing and become champions of decision-making. This book will guide them in this transformation.

# Management summary

The big idea: transforming into a
Decision Oriented Organization

In a world increasingly filled with data, our decisions all become much more explicit. Decisions in the past would often be made, based upon experience, expertise, and intuition. These days, decisions rely increasingly on data; in the world of racing, drivers and team managers compete on the basis of data and decision-supporting models. They are in fact Decision Oriented Organizations, with a dedicated focus on taking the best possible decisions at all times. It has become essential for winning races.

Business leaders can learn from the experiences of the world of racing. In this book we argue that they must transform into Decision Oriented Organizations to remain successful in business, especially in times of chaos and crisis.

One of the main challenges is that business leaders must learn to look at decisions in the same way Formula 1 teams do. They need a new lens. That is precisely why we must first realize that a Decision Oriented Organization has to deal with various types of decisions.

## 1. Types of decisions

A decision has two dimensions:

- First, the speed at which the decision is made (or should be made).
- Second, the impact of the decision.

Plotting these dimensions on two axes creates a simple matrix with four different types of decisions.

|  | Low Speed | High Speed |
|---|---|---|
| High Impact | **Smart scenario** | **Advanced algorithm** |
| Low Impact | **Human decision** | **Business rule** |

Table 0.1 Decision types

## 2. Design principles for a Decision Oriented Organization

With this simple model in hand, leaders can plot the dynamics of their organization –or certain processes or units – and link design principles to them. We can define four different design principles.

Two of these are related to the speed of decisions:

**Autonomy:** If a high decision-making speed is required, it is often not feasible to have the decision made at the top via a strict hierarchical organization. These decisions call for an organization where teams / professionals have the autonomy to make decisions on the spot.

**Level of automation:** In many cases, computers are faster at processing data and calculating scenarios for a decision. That is why high-speed decisions will in many cases require a relatively high degree of automation.

The other two are related to the impact of the decisions:

**Investment.** It goes without saying that every organization should invest mainly in high-impact projects. As little money as possible should be spent on less important matters. And that also applies to decision-making processes: high impact justifies a high investment in resources to improve those processes.

**Reliability.** Every decision requires reliable data and robust business rules or algorithms, but especially in cases of high-impact decisions, nothing should go wrong. High-impact decisions therefore require a great deal of attention to the aspect of reliability.

### The CFO in pole position

The matrix with the types of decisions combined with the four design principles is at the core of transforming into what we call Decision Oriented Organizations, well-oiled information processing machines that continuously deliver state-of-the-art decisions throughout all domains and all organizational levels. It is a new perspective on how to optimize the use of data for excellent decisions, based on the modus operandi within Formula 1 teams.

This book describes the various challenges of applying this perspective. This book also argues that this job is well-suited to CFOs and analyses how they can take up this role with confidence.

# PART 1
# SETTING THE SCENE

The impact of datafication on business and how data can
revolutionize decision-making

# Chapter 1  An old new role for CFOs

Who is managing the store when it
comes to information?

'*Information is a corporate asset to be managed by a
top-ranking executive.*'

This is considered a truth among many experts in an era of
abundant data. It is also a statement in the first international
edition of *CIO Magazine*, published in 1987 (!). At the time,
Chief Information Officers (CIOs) were expected to take on
this role. More than 30 years later, however, many CIOs have
not stepped up to this plate. In practice, many CIOs mainly
play the role of Chief Technology Officer. They have enough
trouble keeping systems up and running, managing costs, and
managing today's myriad cybersecurity risks without worry-
ing about the bigger picture.

Taking the time to rethink how information could be used to
create greater business value appears to be a rather neglected
element.

With fundamental changes taking place in many areas of our
world, this situation no longer seems tenable. More than ever
before, organizations need to take better decisions – based on

better insights – if they are to outperform their competition. And *how* those decisions are being made is also changing – radically (see Table 1.1).

| Old | New |
|---|---|
| Periodic decisions | Ongoing decision-making process |
| People make decisions based on instinct and experience | Machines make decisions based on facts and rules |
| Decisions are made unconsciously | Decisions are made consciously |
| Managers make the decisions (top down) | Everyone makes decisions (bottom up) |
| Decisions are an internal matter | Decisions are made in external ecosystems |

Table 1.1 Overview of changes in decision-making

Back in 1987 (the time of the aforementioned quote in *CIO Magazine*) , companies were hardly thinking about Big Data, Artificial Intelligence, Robotic Process Automation and other innovative digital technology. How very different this is, today. Today, they could not survive without paying strategic attention to those subjects. Managing information is no longer merely a prerequisite for running a successful business – information management IS the business. And it is high time that companies anticipate on this new reality.

They must transform into Decision Oriented Organizations. This is necessary not only because of the huge potential of data (and the blossoming amount of tooling to use this data), it is also necessary to withstand times of chaos and crisis. In the eye of a storm it is more important than ever to have reliable and relevant information at hand for decisions. In 2020, the world faced the COVID-19 coronavirus pandemic. At the time of writing this book, it is too early to tell with certainty which companies have the best responses. Early signs, however, show that frontrunners in data-driven approaches are the ones best prepared for a multitude of challenges posed by COVID-19. They are the ones that can quickly develop scenarios and have the information at hand for swift and powerful anticipations of a new reality, even at a time when this new reality is still fuzzy.

**The CFO in pole position**
This book thoroughly analyses the changes in decision-making (Table 1.1). First, however, it is important to take a closer look at the role of CFOs, as they are best suited to prepare organizations for the new reality.

CFOs were not chosen at random to get this job done. The choice has to do with three unique characteristics of CFOs (and the finance function as a whole). The job of building a Decision Oriented Organization fits them like a glove.

*Characteristic 1: CFOs are impartial*
Traditionally, CFOs have always been the – business economics – conscience of an organization and, therefore, have always filled an impartial role on any executive board. They have a decisive vote in allocating resources to projects (i.e. they are in charge of the money). In doing so, they always needed to rely on the facts without sentiment or prejudice. CFOs are trained to prevent these emotions from playing a role in the assessment of information and to always look for the facts.

*Characteristic 2: CFOs are a connecting link*
Integral, connecting, holistic. These are the key concepts, according to the majority of reports by consultancies, on how organizations should successfully anticipate the digital transformation. And quite rightly so, because the walls should be removed between the traditional compartments of organizations. Here, too, CFOs have the advantage. They are already a connecting link between the various disciplines, and research[2] has shown that the span of control of CFOs is increasing, with people reporting to them from IT to cybersecurity and from risk management to Mergers & Acquisitions. The same research also notes that more than half of all CFOs have responsibilities 'at the forefront of digitization', such as in automation, robotics, data visualization, and artificial intelligence (AI). Increasingly, all support functions (like HR, IT, Finance, Procurement) report to the CFO who thereby has the overarching responsibility to enable a smooth-running primary process.

*Characteristic 3: CFOs understand information*
Last but not least, CFOs are trained to create, analyse, report, distribute, and communicate reliable information. It is at the core of their responsibilities – and always has been. With some imagination we can go back six centuries to the Italian invention of the double-entry bookkeeping system – with a debit and credit side – which is still in use today. In his book *The Reckoning: Financial Accountability and the Rise and Fall of Nations,*[3] US historian Jacob Soll writes about the importance of this invention as a basis of modern capitalism. 'Good accounting practices have produced the levels of trust necessary to fund stable governments and vital capitalist societies, and poor accounting and its attendant lack of accountability

have led to financial chaos, economic crimes, civil unrest, and worse.'

It is also a fact that finance professionals are trained like no other in gathering reliable and verifiable information. Their training includes the processing, categorization, and consolidation of information. In cases of any doubt, they can and will turn to accounting guidelines that provide guidance for the correct categorization of transactions. They set up frameworks with key controls to ensure that information is reliable, and are also familiar with the related Three Lines of Defence (see Chapter 6). In recent decades, financial experts have implemented and refined International Financial Reporting Standards (IFRS) in Europe, in order to improve the comparability of information for the capital market. To this end, they have often had to invest heavily in systems that deliver better information for supervisory bodies. In the financial sector, the same applies to the supervisory frameworks of Solvency II and Basel II, which also ensured better provision of information all based on a combination of very precise definitions and policies on how to register and report on an increasing number of indicators.

**Navigating in the eye of a storm**
The mentioned specific competencies that CFOs have are especially relevant in times of change or crisis as information tends to become notoriously unreliable in these times. The COVID-19 crisis has highlighted this again; various sources offer conflicting information and experts formed their view of what needs to be done based on their information source of

choice. Jevin West and Carl Bergstrom, professors from the University of Washington and founders of an online course called 'Calling Bullshit in Big Data' call such crises a 'natural ecology of bullshit',[4] as such an environment offers psychological and financial rewards for attracting attention regardless of the accuracy and trustworthiness of information. The COVID-19 pandemic soon proved to be a real bonanza for statistics, graphs, and data visualizations of how the virus developed with an overload of questionable information. Fighting incorrect information proved to be a tough cookie for social networks and tech companies such as Twitter or Google.

This is not only true when it comes to societal crises and news media. It's also valid when it comes to being well informed in corporate crises. One of the main objectives in such times is to distinguish crappy or subjective information from reliable and fact-based information, thereby making sure that there is one version of the truth as a solid base for decisions. Cutting through a complex jungle of misinformation is key. And CFOs are well positioned and trained to do this.

## How the CFO can become the architect of the Decision Oriented Organization

The aforementioned three characteristics are typical of many CFOs and other financial professionals. In fact, professionals in other areas, such as human resources (HR), marketing, and logistics, could learn a thing or two from CFOs. Finance departments have, for instance, spent years perfecting elaborate accounting manuals to make sure that everyone speaks the same language when it comes to processing information. To many other professionals this may not be a top priority. For instance: Which HR professional comes up with the idea to define what an FTE (full-time equivalent) is? Or how many sales executive would think of correcting monthly sales statistics for essential elements, such as the number of weekends in a given month?

For many financial professionals, such questions are routine. It is deeply ingrained in the professional ethics of finance professionals to present their organization with the best available information, thus providing peace of mind to the managers who need to be able to rely on such information.

This is an essential skill, particularly in a time when the volume of data is exploding. And so, besides taking the lead in classifying, consolidating, and analysing the financial information, CFOs must also do this for all other types of information. They should become the architects of the Decision Oriented Organization. And they definitely could use some help from other executives.

CFOs need the help of other executives to succeed in this.

First of all, they must team up with the CIO. In the past, there was some doubt about the strategic value of the CIO. In 2013, an analysis in *Harvard Business Review*, with the revealing heading *'Why can't a CIO be more like a CFO?'*, concluded that it is 'time for CIOs to move beyond their role as chief technology officer and embrace the name with all of its implications: Chief *Information* Officer.' The article continues by answering the question of why they are not doing so: 'Because no one is managing the store'.[5] Although the I in CIO stands for *information*, CIOs have not been including this aspect in their responsibilities in recent decades.

This criticism does not alter the fact that CIOs have an incredibly important role in ensuring that the IT landscape – the backbone of any company – is strong and secure. They are essential to enabling organizations to innovate and to build a robust yet flexible IT infrastructure. That is their contribution to building a Decision Oriented Architecture.

Then there is the chief executive officer (CEO). Generally speaking, CEOs have a strategic role and are a company's face to the outside world. The fact that the handling of information is a strategic issue goes without saying. CEOs must therefore be missionaries and communicate clearly and often. They must inspire the organization to make sure that the CFO's work of building a Decision Oriented Organization is well understood.

The following two chapters analyse the impact of the omnipresence of data and the related digital transformation. The main focus is on what will change and what will not, and, subsequently, on what that means for how companies should handle information.

# Chapter 2  Everything changes

## 'Do or die' in a digital era

*Everything changes, at breakneck speed. Although it is a overused cliché, it is nevertheless important to reflect on these changes and the opportunities they present for many executives. There is a justified need for speed, but there is no point in chasing hype – fear of missing out is not the best approach. Let's briefly analyse the undercurrent of how the role of data changes, as this is the basis for avoiding hype.*

In early 2014, the Marriott hotel chain proudly announced plans to offer no fewer than 30,000 new hotel rooms that year. Brian Chesky, CEO and co-founder of Airbnb, promptly responded with a teasing message on Twitter: 'Marriott wants to add 30,000 rooms this year. We will add that in the next 2 weeks'.[6] The message illustrates succinctly how business models are being turned upside down because of the world's rapid digitization.

We see the signs everywhere. Take, for example, today's ranking of the most valuable companies in the world. This list is no longer dominated by oil companies, car companies, and retail giants, but by tech giants (especially new ones) who build business models based on the smart use of data. Another indication is the fact that many politicians and executives are concerned about the global power of the so-called Frightful Five – Microsoft, Alphabet, Facebook, Apple, and Amazon – although this grossly ignores the large influence of Chinese data giants such as Alibaba, Tencent, and Baidu, as their influence is less visible in the West.

## How new kids on the block define business

One glance at the list of unicorns – privately owned start-ups valued at over US$ 1 billion – provides a similar picture. This list consists mainly of companies using digital business models. And a similar picture emerges if we look at companies in the next category just below those unicorns. According to Statistics Netherlands (CBS)[7], the Netherlands hit a record in 2018, with over 10,000 fast-growing companies that year. These companies showed an annual 10% growth in terms of personnel for three consecutive years, starting with at least 10 employees in the base year. Many of these companies have timed the wave of digitization well. A similar picture can be seen in many other countries.

Technology companies are certainly not the only ones riding that wave. This is also and emphatically the case in the financial sector, for example. For a number of years now, innovative front runners among the banks have been applying a platform strategy; activities that have a profound impact on the organization and go well beyond appearances. Dutch financial institution ING is one example of this. Speaking at a banking conference in 2018, ING CEO Ralph Hamers demonstrated how he improved his bank's position within the banking sector: 'The banks of the future are open. Open to individual users and producers. Open to third parties that provide complementary goods and services. Open to the competition'.[8] This is a world away from how banks operated only a decade ago.

### Information hubs have a strong future

Business models are being turned upside down in just about every sector. The Port of Rotterdam has abandoned its goal of wanting to become the largest in the business; instead, it now strives to be the smartest. To succeed in this endeavour, the port needs to turn itself into a logistics information hub where goods and data are handled equally smoothly. It does not take much imagination to envisage a situation in the not too distant future where consumers are able to follow a ship that contains some product they ordered from China, in real time, as it makes its way across the oceans. In fact, a programme manager is quoted saying, 'Information which is now transmitted between humans by phone or email should, from 2025, be increasingly communicated directly by smart objects. In the future, we'll see cranes talking directly to ships or containers.'[9]

Every sector will be affected, including those with physical products at the core of their business. Although it is safe to say that a bag of potatoes will never crawl through a fibre-optic cable, creating value with these potatoes is, in fact, increasingly a matter of smart data handling.

The wave of technology may be overwhelming to some managers and business leaders. Rushed responses to this wave of change are often not the best course of action for them. Companies that understand the underlying forces are better able to consistently anticipate these changes. With this in mind, we zoom in on how business models develop over time.

### How business models have evolved historically

A brief look at history reveals the models that were created over time. Research by OpenMatters and Deloitte divides industries into separate groups according to four models.[10]

1. Asset Builders. These companies use physical assets to create and/or market their products. Examples are car manufacturers, chemical plants, airlines, and retailers.
2. Service Providers. These companies hire staff to provide certain services to customers in exchange for payment. Examples are consultancy firms and financial institutions.
3. Technology Creators. These companies develop and sell intellectual property such as software, analytics, pharmaceutical products, and biotechnology.
4. Network Orchestrators. These companies create and maintain networks for participants to meet and enter into transactions. These networks include digital marketplaces, social media platforms, and online dating sites.

The historical developments of these four models reveal the underlying, at that time new, technology.

Asset Builders, for example, are the product of the Industrial Revolution. The rise of the steam engine enabled the switch to efficient mass production.

Service Providers emerged particularly in the 1970s.

The rise of the Technology Creators cannot be separated from the information revolution of the 1990s, which resulted from rapidly developing computer technology and the rise of the Internet.

And the most recent development: the emergence of the Network Orchestrators. It originated from a combination of technological developments such as cloud computing, social networks, Internet of Things, and, last but certainly not least: the smartphone. Below, we elaborate on these 'new kids on the block', also known as platform companies. Not because they have become the poster children of the business world, but because they operate according to completely different dynamics, as their way of processing information is what sets them apart from the competition. They are, in fact, examples of Decision Oriented Organizations.

First, we analyse how these platform companies are extremely data driven.

Second, we analyse the high market valuations of these companies.

### Network Orchestrators excel in data-driven decisions
There are numerous types of Network Orchestrators, but essentially they all do the same thing. They don't own assets, but rather link the supply and demand of products and services. They usually operate on a large scale, are strongly data driven, and apply digital tools to excel in efficiency, speed, and/or hyper-personalization.

These companies do not create value within the walls of their own organizations but do so within an ecosystem. Front-runners in competitive markets are no longer the companies who control the physical resources, but those who are the best at matching supply and demand, down to the individual level. It is about excelling in information processing. As described in

Deloitte's paper *The rise of the platform economy*, the strength of the platform economy lies in its ability to eliminate trade barriers by taking advantage of the increase in information sharing between various players and the circulation of data.[11]

The impact of the rise of the Network Orchestrators can hardly be overestimated – among other things, because of the unpredictability of the competition which can suddenly appear from anywhere. Value, after all, can be created using other people's assets.

Chinese Internet company Alibaba is an example of this. It does not need physical outlets or warehouses to compete with US retail chain Walmart; all it needs to do is rent some additional server space. Uber is also a clear example of how this works in practice. At first glance, Uber may appear to be a taxi company, but in reality, it is an information processing platform where supply and demand are matched. Without buying as much as a single taxi cab itself, the company could potentially gain enormous power over the taxi world. It is a completely different form of value creation than in the old economy. The value lies in the act of connecting, whereas in the old model, this would be seen as overhead costs. In this way, Network Orchestrators create a market for themselves without competition. In the words of Silicon Valley techno guru Peter Thiel in an opinion piece in the *Wall Street Journal*: 'Competition is for losers'.[12]

And we ain't seen nothin' yet, if experts are to be believed. Consumer markets will not be the only sectors where such platform companies take dominant positions. For consumer markets, the advent of the smartphone was essential; it ensured that people were online almost all the time and that transactions could be processed more efficiently than ever before. Without the smartphone, platforms such as Uber and Airbnb would never have been so enormously successful.

Experts believe the next wave of platforms will focus on business-to-business sectors. This time, explosive growth will not be driven by the smartphone but by the Internet of Things. For the logistics sector, the multitude of sensors in an unbelievably wide variety of appliances will, for example, link supply and demand with great precision and speed. According to Sangeet Choudary, one of the prominent thinkers in this field, 'Many parts of the industrial economy already apply the marketplace model. For example, different parts of the logistics chain, ranging from trucking fleets to container ships, have built platforms to match spare capacity with demand, in an Uber-like system for heavy industry logistics. However, these systems are only partially effective because they still need to plug into a traditional supply chain. With increasing digitization, a digitized manufacturing process could interact with a digitized logistics system, lending itself to greater coordination across the end-to-end supply chain. This is when large-scale network effects can be unlocked on B2B platforms'.[13]

### Network Orchestrators get valued highly in capital markets

There is also a great financial impact from the emergence of new business models according to the aforementioned Deloitte analysis. For 40 years, companies that embrace new technology and create digital networks can count on increasingly higher financial market valuations. These days, their value is determined more often than not by intangible factors rather than tangible assets. In the case of network orchestrators – platform companies such as Uber and Spotify – value is determined by their ability to use data in optimizing interactions between participants.

The analysis also puts a number on it: the multipliers are two to four times higher in the valuation of Technology Creators and Network Orchestrators than those of traditional Asset Builders and Service Providers. This is already impressive, while, for the newest generation of Network Orchestrators, the figures are even many times higher. Many ratings have gone so high that critics are wondering whether they will be justified by future profits in the long term. And this is also why music platform Spotify's figures are critically monitored in the media. Spotify is undoubtedly a very successful platform with hundreds of millions of subscribers worldwide, but it is also true that this platform company has yet to find the magic wand that will create the substantial profits in the future that would justify its current rating of dozens of billions of euros.

**How new business models shine a new light on the role of CFOs**
This shift in business models has a huge impact on CFOs, as it is affects their responsibilities in four areas:

1 Adjustments to the allocation of capital
2 Relationships with investors
3 Shifts in mental models
4 Mastering the data.

In the first place, the role of the CFO includes responsibility for **adjusting capital allocation**. Capital must be applied where it creates the most value. As Deloitte's analysis shows, many traditional companies have not changed much in this area over the past 40 years. It is up to CFOs to ensure that at least part of the company's capital investment ends up in projects and programmes aimed at achieving new business models. Although this is an important task, to be sure, it is one that is only partially covered in the scope of this book.

Secondly, the business models transformation also impacts **investor relations**, as valuation will not increase until investors understand how the new business models work. Introducing and explaining these new models often calls for different ways of providing information to investors, including different key performance indicators (KPIs). This is a task for CFOs. In Chapter 6, we will analyse how the nature of both management information and external reporting changes.

For CFOs, the third area of responsibility relates to **shifting mental models**. The Deloitte analysis concludes that 'Companies, through their leaders, invest in what they believe has value, and that is driven by the "mental model" of a company's CEO, the CFO, its management team, and board of directors. For example, leaders of Asset Builders believe that value resides in developing and owning or leasing hard assets, which can be used for manufacturing, distributing, and selling physical things. On the other hand, Network Orchestrators' top priorities are building and operating social and commercial networks that foster interactions and co-creation with their customers and suppliers.' This hits the nail on the head. Taking the step towards a new business model can only succeed if the company's management (1) fully understands how that business model works and (2) is actually convinced of its possibilities. Here, CFOs are the agents of change, a role discussed in more detail in Chapter 8 of this book.

The fourth and final aspect is that of **mastering the data**. Network orchestrators will only be able to marry supply and demand if they have the data to do so – efficiently and with surgical precision. Which is why they do everything in their power to maintain data quality, ensure smooth data access, and derive valuable insights and prognoses from them. In an ideal world, they should be able to anticipate the needs of customers, rather than respond to them.[14] The notion that data mastering would mainly be about building large 'data lakes', improving ERP systems, and/or using innovative tools for data analysis is a major misunderstanding. Although these items are all strategic, 'mastering' data goes beyond tooling. It is also about the use of unstructured information and connecting internal and external data sources, with fostering a shared belief in data and data quality being among the central elements of competition. It is also about a new relationship between humans and machines in data-driven decision-making processes, and many other factors that play a role, here. All these factors are at the heart of building a Decision Oriented Organization and thus also at the heart of this book. Mastering the data is in fact the main topic of Chapter 6.

This book provides CFOs with ideas to successfully fulfil the expectations in the aforementioned domains. But, first, it is important to apply some nuance to the pace of change in the next chapter.

# Chapter 3   Even in times of radical change, some things will remain the same

Relevance will always be key to successful entrepreneurship

*As we discussed in the previous chapter, a changing world is fuelling the evolution of business models. We are facing an impressive wave of innovations which CFOs will need to anticipate. But it is also important to note that some things never change.*

An article in 2015 quotes Amazon CEO Jeff Bezos saying how he was often asked about what he believed was going to change over the next decade, but that hardly anyone ever asked him about which things are likely to remain the same. According to Bezos, the answer to this second question represents the more important vision, as it is much better to build strategies on certainties rather than on uncertainties.[15]

Bezos, of course, has a valid point. His example: customers want low prices and good service, which is unlikely to change in 10 years' time. Generally, we could say that extreme expectations are the new normal and are here to stay. Fuelled by fantastic technology, customers expect to be able to operate every application intuitively and simply, require it to never fail, and, preferably, to be free of charge.

## Move with the times

Bezos's way of thinking also confirms the age-old wisdom that relevance is the only basis for entrepreneurial success. It should therefore be the starting point for organizations wanting to become future-proof for the digital era. These days, there is no lack of urgency on this point. For many markets, the pressure is immense. As a result, many organizations have become so-called burning platforms, where the need for change is felt by everyone. Nevertheless, the drive for change is not always fully recognized in practice, and often generates counterproductive reflexes.

There are many examples of things that went wrong. For instance, streaming media technology totally disrupted many business models in the entertainment industry. One of the victims was Blockbuster, at the time a large chain of video stores in the US market. In 2013, the plug was pulled on this company as its prospects for the future had disappeared – not because Blockbuster's management recognized how streaming services were changing the market, but because it was unable to incorporate the new technology into its own business model and remain relevant to customers. Netflix, however, proved able to 'move with the times' like no other, which is why it became the big winner in this sector.[16]

Blockbuster represents only one of the many examples of very popular companies that were unable to adapt when technology turned their market on its head. The Eastman Kodak Company (Kodak), in the end, was unable to keep up with digital camera developments. Nokia suffered the same fate with the smartphone (and more specifically the success of platform thinking around the smartphone). And there are many more of such illustrative cases. It is also important to point out that many of these companies were in fact very much aware of the trends in their market, but they were nevertheless unable to respond effectively with the skills they possessed. Kodak did have the technology for digital photography, but was too hesitant and afraid to make the very necessary yet very severe change of course. When developing their mobile telephones, Nokia continued its strategy of focusing on quality even though they knew very well that the competition would increasingly be about offering the best platform.

### Sinning against the principle

Looking at many of these cases in the rear-view mirror reveals that entrepreneurial demise started when these companies disregarded the principle key to success: *relevance.* Prominent researchers and management book authors in this field also point this out from various perspectives.

First, there is Simon Sinek and his famous book *Start with Why*.[17] In it, he distinguishes three 'Golden circles': What, How, and Why. Many companies appear to only know *what* they offer the market and *how* they do this. Few can say *why* they do the things the way they do. Companies that can, however, are able to really appeal to customers and connect with them. Success – financial and otherwise – follows almost automatically. This mindset offers an important lesson to leaders who are serious about starting a transition process. They must be able to answer the question of *why*. When responding to digitization, it is essential that employees are aware of their organization's higher ambitions. And it is precisely this perspective that often is lacking.

Another prominent researcher is the late Clayton Christensen. After years of research, he came to a conclusion that fits in nicely with the above.[18] Professor at Harvard Business School and an authority in the field of innovation, his thought-provoking statements challenge a deep-rooted assumption. Many people believe that understanding the customer is crucial for innovation. But, according to Christensen's reasoning, this assumption is largely incorrect because, as he sees it, customers do not buy a drill, they buy a hole in the wall. In fact, they are buying a solution for hanging a painting. Therefore, rather than knowing the customers themselves, a successful organization should know exactly what problems they are looking to solve. Only then can such companies be and remain relevant. This is particularly true in times of major technological change. Customers are a very poor source of inspiration for innovation, because the majority is unable to imagine how new technology could help them. Thus has it always been; a few hundred years ago, a survey among candle buyers asking for their ideas and possible innovations would probably have revealed a strong need for a less dripping or smouldering candle. It is unlikely that any of them would have come up with an idea for an incandescent lamp. Here, too, the following applies: analysis goes first, as relevance precedes success.

A third prominent thinker in this area is Harvard professor Michael Porter. Particularly interesting is his 'conversion'. For a long time, he was an ardent supporter of the importance of shareholder value. Around 2011, however, he changed his mind quite drastically with his opinion on the new concept of shared value[19]: '... It will also respect capitalism and its relationship to society. Perhaps most important of all, learning how to create shared value is our best chance to legitimise business again.' He now believes that the company of the future will be built on the concept of 'shared value', by contributing to profits and at the same time responding to the needs of stakeholders. In other words, it starts with relevance.

In fact, all these ideas seem to have gained traction in the last years, fuelled by an intensified public and political debate on climate change (and on a sustainable future for our planet in general). More and more, companies realize that they must balance interests from multiple stakeholders. The traditional focus on profit maximization is changing as customers increasingly demand sustainable and fair products – this has become relevant to them. This also implies that the process of decision- making is not only about the best business models and how to achieve operational excellence; sustainability has also become relevant and thereby a key dimension in decision-making.

Why is this analysis of being relevant needed in a book on building a Decision Oriented Organization?

For two reasons:

*1. Exploring beyond the hype*
First of all because relevance is an essential basis for assessing which new digital technology is --and which technology is not – vital to use.

Successfully anticipating and responding to digitization starts with defining relevance. This is Step 1. Once this has been clearly defined, the pathway to continued value creation can be determined. Step 2. Only after these two steps have been completed can the result be translated into choices about purchasing or developing technology. Step 3.

Unfortunately in practice these steps are often taken the other way around. With everyone talking about the latest technology at conferences and workshops, managers feel pressured and afraid to miss out. The shiny objects dangled before their eyes are very tempting and cause them to proceed to allocate funds to acquire certain technology without having a good idea of how it would contribute to their company's relevance. Even more unfortunately, in certain instances these managers hesitate to question technology sellers about their product or fail to talk to experts inside and outside their organization for fear that people will think they are stupid. We will dig into this more in detail in Chapter 7.

## 2. Information processing as basis for relevance

Second, relevance is important in relation to the wise words from Jeff Bezos, on building a strategy on what's certain in business. This will be different for every company, but one certainty in today's world full of data is that the best possible methods of data processing, enrichment, and use for decision-making are a strong basis for remaining relevant. Because taking better decisions than your peers will make a difference now and in the future. That is why it's so important to understand the fundamentals of a Decision Oriented Organization.

In the following chapter, we analyse more in depth how Formula 1 teams are Decision Oriented Organizations with a strong focus on maximizing insights from data. There are great parallels between this world and the business community, which is why valuable lessons can be learned from comparing them.

# Chapter 4  It's the data, stupid!

What businesses could learn from data-driven
decision-making in Formula 1

*In the world of racing, drivers and team managers used to
base their decisions on a combination of experience, expertise, and intuition. This is no longer the case. Today, they
increasingly do so on the basis of hard data and advanced
models: they have transformed into Decision Oriented Organizations. There are valuable lessons to be learned from
this for the business community.*

Winning a Formula 1 Grand Prix without the benefit of
high-quality data analysis has become nearly inconceivable.
To the fans, data strategy is all but invisible, but behind the
scenes, competition is thwarted through effective interpretation of the data; data on engine performance, wear and tear of
the tyres, cloud formation over the racetrack, and how these
relate to the strategy for a particular race, to name but a few.
Whether, for example, an 'undercut' (i.e. a cleverly timed early
pit stop[20]) is a sensible strategy is determined by mathemati-
cal models using live data rather than by a human being.

As such, Formula 1 is playing in the proverbial Champions
League of data analysis.

The devil is in the detail, especially when a fraction of a second can make the difference, as it does in motorsports. The Chief Information Officer at Red Bull Racing described how each season data analysis leads to as many as 30,000 large and small changes to the car[21] to maximize its racing performance. The important role of data collection was, for example, demonstrated in 2018, when the Formula 1 circus arrived in Austin, Texas. Heavy rains flooded the track and put an end to the Friday training sessions. The teams had barely been able to collect any data, and their racing strategies were more of a leap of faith than actual strategies. For example, none of the teams had had the opportunity to test their slicks – tyres for dry conditions. This unusual situation caused the Sunday race to enter the books as a magnificent and spectacular battle and with large differences between the strategies of the top teams. For the unbiased spectators, this was a real treat compared to many of the other races which are often rather predictable – much to the chagrin of many motorsport enthusiasts.

## The genie is out of the bottle

For Ross Brawn, managing and technical director of Formula 1, the impact of the incident in Austin led him to ponder whether such a spectacle could not be realized more often by introducing a restriction on the use of data. He compared this with a football match: if two teams both play a technically perfect game, the result would be a 0-0 tie. But that is not what spectators come to see. The key question, according to him, is whether less data leads to a better show. According to him that is the real question since less predictability could make the sport more attractive for spectators going forward. When asked, Toto Wolff, team principal and CEO of the Mercedes AMG Petronas Motorsport Formula 1 Team – one of the top

that data and algorithms were used in making certain decisions is very transparent or can be made transparent. Contrary to popular belief, an algorithm is not always a black box: its decisions can actually better be explained than those of the supposedly inimitable human brain.[24]

Businesses are greatly attracted to the promise of better decisions that come with the use of this data-driven technology – but this does not happen automatically.

Similarly to the Formula 1 driver and his team, in business you need to have a large amount of reliable data at your disposal. Formula 1 teams collect relevant data by mounting sensors on any element that is likely to provide this data and, in order to succeed, you will need to do the same for your organization.

You will also need the best analysis of that data (and therefore the best algorithms). In racing, it takes a substantial knowledge of mathematics and data analysis to make optimal adjustments, for instance, to a racing car's front wing, or to accurately predict the degree of wear of the tyres in a certain race. Winning a race requires smart algorithms in combination with expert analysts.

This is also true when it comes to entrepreneurial success.

Anyone who makes optimal use of data to make better decisions has a real competitive advantage. It is about 'competing on analytics'[25] in the words of author Thomas Davenport, or 'from Big Data to Big Information' and 'the CFO as a decision machine' in the words of Jan Kees de Jager, former Dutch minister of finance and later CFO at KPN.[26]

Here, learning from experience gained in Formula 1 is an obvious course of action. Formula 1 has always been a breeding ground for the type of new technology that would often be introduced some years later in the mass production of cars, from all kinds of safety components to fuel-saving techniques such as storage of the energy that is released during braking. Formula 1 is also becoming a source of inspiration for data-driven decision-making in the business community as the teams have evolved into Decision Oriented Organizations.[27]

## Hypercompetition

The parallel between the world of Formula 1 and the corporate world can also be seen in another aspect. Now that decisions are made more explicitly on the basis of data, hypercompetition emerges. Differences are becoming smaller and smaller. Making a profit is actually becoming more difficult for businesses, precisely because of these diminishing differences. The way the rain prevented those training sessions in Austin illustrates, albeit anecdotally, how this works in Formula 1 racing. If data analysis cannot be performed at the highest level for whatever reason (in this case a long downpour), differences suddenly become substantial again.

Paradoxically, differences will increase when looking at it from another perspective. Because what is also very clear in Formula 1 is the degree of disadvantage suffered by teams that are unable to handle such a challenge and thus are confronted with the fact that they are lagging far behind. There is a good reason for there being only three teams[28] – racing teams of car manufacturers with deep pockets – in front of the rest. The differences between these three are extremely small, whereas the gap with the rest – the laggards – is very large. This can also be seen in the business world. Becoming a Decision Oriented Organization is therefore of the utmost importance: failing to transform may ultimately put you out of business completely. Soon, every decision will be the explicit result of data analysis. In the past, you were able to quickly check the warehouse to see if a product was in stock, but these days you need to rely on the information provided by your systems and/or systems of others. It will not be long before this simple fact applies to literally every decision. Deliveroo and Uber are examples of businesses that fully manage their staff by using data-based algorithms; web shops buy advertising space in a fully auto-mated way, with prices for certain keywords subject to change in a matter of seconds. In such a world, there are simply no other choices. Those who want to be successful must excel in information processing. They must transform into Decision Oriented Organizations because this is increasingly the pre-requisite for success.

In the following chapter, we briefly explain what this new re-ality is about. Subsequent chapters indicate, per theme, how CFOs are able to contribute to building this Decision Orient-ed Organization.

# Chapter 5  Turbocharging Frederick Taylor

Why we need Decision Oriented Organizations

*In a world full of data, decisions are made in a different manner. But exactly what does this new reality entail? This question needs to be answered before we can define the nature of the Decision Oriented Organization.*

*Hey Siri, can you invest my life savings?*[29] In the article 'The rise of the financial machines', *The Economist* describes the increasing importance of machines in the world of asset management, and – with a certain sense of drama – concludes that human investors are about to discover they are no longer the smartest kids on the block. A new reality is indeed emerging when it comes to making decisions. And asset management is not alone in this respect. We see it happening in all domains of society.

Chapter 1 briefly outlined the changing dynamics of decision-making, summarized in table 5.1:

| Old | New |
|---|---|
| Periodic decisions | Ongoing decision-making process |
| People make decisions based on instinct and experience | Machines make decisions based on facts and rules |
| Decisions are made unconsciously | Decisions are made consciously |
| Managers make the decisions (top down) | Everyone makes decisions (bottom up) |
| Decisions are an internal matter | Decisions are made in external ecosystems |

Table 5.1 Overview of changes in decision-making

These elements are further elaborated in this chapter.

*From periodic decisions to an ongoing decision-making process*
In a traditional management cycle, those in charge periodically examine the management reports and, where necessary, adjust operations accordingly. In the new volatile reality, they need to keep a finger on the pulse at all times and make decisions as and when needed.

*From people making decisions based on instinct and experience to machines making decisions based on facts and rules*
People are hopelessly bad at making decisions, partly because they can be irrational, which means they may look at the facts through rose-coloured glasses. But they are also bad at it because they are not inclined to allow room for advancing insights if those are contrary to their own opinions. Machines are much better at doing those things. Moreover, humans tend to base their decisions on historic patterns, which often have lost relevance.

*From unconscious decisions to conscious decisions*
Human decisions are based on a combination of experience, expertise, and intuition. The profession of manager is currently considered one that requires skill, but not one with a clear basis for decision-making. Nor is it always obvious whether individual decisions are good decisions. This situation is changing. Decisions are becoming increasingly explicit.

*From managers making decisions (top down) to everyone making decisions (bottom up)*
Gone are the days when every decision was made by the manager; instead, decisions are increasingly made in the lower echelons of an organization – this process is faster and better.

*From decisions being an internal matter to decisions being made within external ecosystems*
Organizational boundaries are blurring and companies are primarily turning into a collection of interfaces with other organizations. This also means that decisions are made more in conjunction with other parties. A simple example of this is the way suppliers take decisions on stock levels at the retailer warehouses they supply.

**History is repeating itself**
The increasing role of data-driven technology is the next evolutionary phase in organizations but, in a way, history is also repeating itself. During the Industrial Revolution, US engineer Frederick Taylor[30] developed a systematic approach to managing employees, with the aim of organizing production as efficiently as possible. His thinking was very influential in the twentieth century – but was gradually met with increasing criticism.

In a sense, the Taylor approach is more than a century later re-emerging in a more rigid form, at a number of strongly data-driven companies such as Deliveroo and Uber, but this time based purely on data. This data-driven approach can sometimes take on extreme proportions. Software company BetterWorks offers software applications that allow groups of employees to collaborate on setting each other's targets. An app on their smartphones shows them, in real time, how other group members are contributing. In other words, real-time performance measurement. If taken to the extreme, employees become a slave to the continuous assessment process. Or, in the words of *The Economist*, become 'the quantified serf'.[31]

In addition to these examples of operational decisions, there are also those of strategic decisions being uncompromisingly based on facts and figures. Consider, if you like, how managers and directors are increasingly relying on benchmarking their organization against the competition to determine how they are performing.

We could summarize the innovations in data-driven technology in racing terms and speak of a 'turbocharged Taylor' approach. At the time of the Industrial Revolution, Taylor's approach was about dealing with labour as efficiently as possible. In the twenty-first century, Decision Oriented Organizations add efficient and effective data management to this. Whoever is best at adopting this will make the best decisions and, therefore, become tomorrow's winner. The world of Formula 1 has proven this during numerous races. Businesses will have to follow suit quickly if they want to remain successful.

The question is of course: how?

In its most simple form. it boils down to two dimensions .

In this chapter, we distinguished five major developments that prove that building a Decision Oriented Organization is not a nice to have but a must have for executives. One quick glance at the factors shows that the process of decision-making is speeding up. A second glance shows that there is much at stake when it comes to improving decision-making. These two factors – speed and impact – are therefore the logical two dimensions of the matrix we presented in Chapter 1 and that will be subject to deeper exploration in Chapter 7.

Speed and impact will also be important topics in assessing how we can build Decision Oriented Organizations. The following three chapters centre around this question, addressing the following themes: governance (Chapter 6), decision-making (Chapter 7), and organization (Chapter 8).

### Artificial intelligence: vessel for the new communism?

In his book *Homo Deus*, Yuval Noah Harari makes a rather daring statement claiming that capitalism not only has defeated communism because it was superior in an ethical sense or because individual freedoms are such a great asset, but also because of another reason. 'Capitalism has won the Cold War because distributed data processing works better than centralised data processing.' In other words, because it was better at processing data. He adds a befitting anecdote, which incidentally may be an urban legend. The story concerns a visit by one of Mikhail Gorbachov's top officials to London, in the 1990s. In the Soviet Union, with centrally managed markets, the minister of economic affairs would decide how many loaves of bread had to be baked and how much they should cost in the bakeries. Yet, there always were long bread queues at those bakeries. During his visit, the top official wanted to talk to the person in charge of London's bread supply. This person had to be very good at his job, he assumed, as there were no bread queues anywhere. He could not imagine that it was London's self-regulating bread market that took care of efficient planning and pricing and, thus, ensured a well-balanced market – the capitalist system proved to be better at processing information.

Now that over 30 years have passed, we may ask whether there is a better alternative to the 'invisible hand' of self-regulating markets, with all their data and smart tooling. To readers who think this sounds a little far-fetched, the words of Jack Ma (founder of the Alibaba group), spoken during a speech in 2017, should be considered. Jack Ma thinks that we may have such a better alternative, now that huge amounts of data allow us to get an unprecedented in-depth and very detailed understanding of how markets work. A centrally managed operation using Artificial Intelligence would function better than self-regulation to increase the efficiency of local markets.[32] In the past, centrally managed communist operations simply lacked the close details needed to process this information properly, but this problem could be solved with today's technology. This would have all sorts of consequences (which are outside the scope of this book). According to some, Artificial Intelligence heralds the end of capitalism in its present form.[33] In any case, data – the fuel for Artificial Intelligence – clearly offers a wealth of decision-making possibilities for market introductions and pricing; things that many of today's companies are only able to dream about.

# PART 2
# THREE DOMAINS OF CHANGE

On a new reality when it comes to governance,
decision-making and organization

# Chapter 6  Governance

FROM
having a grip on financial data
TO
having a grip on all data processing

*Decision-making is increasingly data driven – on all organizational levels. Consequently, using reliable data and ensuring algorithms work correctly becomes more and more essential. This goes far beyond mere financial data. What can the CFO do to govern a broader spectrum of data and data processes?*

On 7 June 2012, John Galvin appeared before a Senate committee in the United States on behalf of the Bureau of Labor Statistics. The committee wanted an explanation of the definition of a 'green' job and, more specifically, about an implemented change in that definition. It turned out to be a rather painful session. Galvin, visibly annoyed, had to admit in front of the committee that bus drivers, gas station attendants, sales people in second-hand record shops, and Salvation Army employees, among others, qualified as workers in green jobs. Towards the end of the session, things became even more painful when the committee asked: 'How about oil lobbyists? Wouldn't being an oil lobbyist count as a green job if they're engaged in advocacy related to environmental issues?' The answer was 'Yes', as even those who worked for oil lobbying firms had a job that could be defined as 'green' according to the definition.[34]

This example shows the importance of definitions, also with respect to data. If policymakers are relying on data that also cause oil lobbyists to be regarded as having a green job, this does not bode well for any of their other decisions, to put it mildly. Data reliability is important and goes much further than a flawed definition. Unreliability may also result from poor data sources, statistical errors, or deliberate deception. The sagacious quotes about this are as numerous as they are revealing. The British economist Ronald Coase once said, 'If you torture the data long enough, they will confess'.[35] US Professor Aaron Levenstein compared statistics to a bikini: 'Statistics are like a bikini: what they reveal is suggestive, but what they conceal is vital'.[36] And then there is the famous statement: 'There are lies, damned lies, and statistics',[37] a quote that (never with certainty) has been attributed to British politician Benjamin Disraeli.

This is not a book about statistics but rather about how CFOs could help their organizations excel in data processing in order to make better decisions. One of the things that needs to be addressed, in any case, is that strict data governance is the basis of those decisions.

### Governance is about mastering the data

Governance, in this context, means a proper monitoring and control of data, definitions, statistical models, reporting structures and the like, with the aim of using the available data in a controlled way, to result in the best possible decisions. This does not mean that 100% certainty is required in

all cases. However, what it should do is provide peace of mind
– something that calls for sufficient confidence about data
quality, use of all the possibilities, and related tooling offered
by such data.

In other words, it's about mastering the data.
As mentioned before, there is much at stake; when things are
not in order, organizations are at risk of making the wrong
decisions and losing to the competition. Good governance is
therefore not a matter of 'good bookkeeping because this is
required' but of 'being and staying in control because that is
what matters'. In line with this, being in charge of governance
will become one of the most appealing roles within an organization and is a crucial one for superior decision-making.

**Which roles should CFO play?**
The good news is that CFOs and their teams are the undisput-
ed champions of such governance, as also argued in Chapter
1. They are trained like no other in their field, in general and
in managing reliable data processing. And they are in an independent position, which enables them to fulfil this role successfully. This is precisely why CFOs deserve a leading role in
this area. This chapter divides their role into three tasks.

*Move data governance from the basement into the boardroom
(6.1)*
Data governance is not a department but rather a basic attitude. The entire organization needs to be aware of what is
at stake. Data is the fuel for making the best decisions and,
therefore, for the success of the organization as a whole. So, it
is up to CFOs to manage data quality and act as missionaries
to involve the entire organization. Because it matters.

*Make sure you understand the story behind the data (6.2)*
As they are often better at it, systems that analyse data are increasingly taking over the role of decision maker previously held by humans. This concerns both simple and easy to explain rule-based algorithms and more complex applications of artificial intelligence. The results do hold certain new types of risks. CFOs, therefore, must take the lead in supervising the soundness of the analyses produced by those systems. If we expect systems to find better answers with data, humans have to learn to ask the right questions.

*Do not be afraid to standardize (6.3)*
Information systems are often tailored to the specific requirements and wishes of an organization. This may sound like a positive, but in many cases it is unnecessary and leads to implementation problems. It also causes delays and failures. Increased standardization of both processes and information systems enhances the exchange of information and provides a breeding ground for new technology, such as robotization. It is also a prerequisite for proper data governance.

In this chapter, we will now offer a more in-depth analysis of these three tasks.

## 6.1   Move data governance from the basement into the boardroom

*Many organizations are living with an inherited IT structure that struggles to satisfy modern informational demand. Some organizations run hundreds of applications, some of which are over 30 years old. This is one of the reasons why businesses are*

*unable to supply reliable and unambiguous data to feed algo-*
*rithms and make decisions. It's one of the factors blocking the*
*way to becoming a Decision Oriented Organization.*

*This is increasingly causing distress in a world that is data driv-*
*en, where success depends on having the best insights. More and*
*more funds are directed to raising the quality of data albeit with*
*often disappointing results. Currently, data quality projects fre-*
*quently come down to 'repair after the fact'.*

*The large amount of attention paid to data quality often origi-*
*nates from a negative perspective. An organization's willingness*
*to invest is based on wanting to prevent bad data from leading to*
*errors and/or reputation damage. A much better line of reason-*
*ing would be one that looks at the value that could be generated.*
*This is where learnings from Formula 1 are important: Formula*
*1 teams invest in data governance because they are convinced*
*it will help them win races, not primarily to prevent errors. In*
*business, we should follow the same line of reasoning.*

Some years ago, the executive board of an insurance company realized how immensely important data quality was becoming in light of the digital transformation of the insurance
sector. After all, good quality data enabled them not only to
better serve their clients but also to start up digital innovations – mostly in the field of customer experience – at short
notice, take the best possible decisions, and create flexibility
in responding to calls for information. The insurance company started a process of ambitious improvements, the importance of which was communicated from the top. Then a
sufficiently large budget was made available, and a substantial
number of professionals were appointed to get this job done.

The project was bursting with energy and later was celebrated as a roaring success.

Two years later, they were right back where they started.

The disappointed management commissioned an assessment of how this could have happened. One of the conclusions was that attention to data quality had been a temporary add-on rather than having been fully embedded in the organization. The assessment also gave insights into seemingly small but nonetheless vital shortcomings. For example, the customer service department had neglected to check and update client data whenever there was customer contact via phone or chat. The customer service staff could hardly be blamed for this fact, as they had been specifically instructed to be as efficient as possible. Checking and updating data takes time and this did not fit well into the amount of time call centre staff were allowed to spend on individual customers.

### Rushing to invest in data quality

There is no lack of attention to the issue of data quality amongst a majority of managers and executives. And there is also no lack of awareness that they are dealing with a fragmented and complex IT world. In that world, a uniform way of registering, processing, and aggregating data is often lacking and workarounds are common practice. IT managers hate to admit it, but many organizations are still using a wide variety of Excel applications, whereby data from source systems is downloaded into Excel and, after processing, uploaded into the source system again... with all the obvious risks of errors that this entails.

Against this background, a myriad of approaches have mush-roomed, under various names, to help solve the problem of poor data, often supported by a wide variety of consultants on Master Data Management, Data Stewardship, Data Quality, Data Governance, and Industry Data Governance, just to name a few. This book uses the term Data Governance, because it reflects the fact that there is an organization-wide and ongoing responsibility to work on data improvement. It is an umbrella term for managing data availability, quality, and integrity. And it requires investing in people, processes, and technology.

As is often the case, there is no uniform interpretation of the definition of data governance. Much more important than the definition is the question of how structural improvements could best be achieved.

## Change the lifestyle

Here, a comparison can be made with people wanting to lose weight. A few months of dieting in combination with a gym routine will probably yield significant results. However, we all know that such effects are temporary unless certain lifestyle changes are made. Long-term success can only be achieved by those who truly believe that a change in lifestyle will make their lives better and healthier. The example of the insurance company illustrates how many companies are addressing data quality as a separate issue that can be considered in isolation. One could say that they had gone on a diet without making any other lifestyle changes.

## Consequences of inadequate data

If an organization's data is not in order, many things can go wrong. Below, we provide a number of examples from everyday practice.

After years of complete radio silence, an organization sent out a message to one of its customers. Unfortunately, the person to whom it was addressed had died a number of years previously. Although, at the time, the customer's death had been entered into the system, the information appeared to have been lost during a subsequent conversion of that system. Something like this is not only awkward but also harms the organization's reputation, as these types of painful incidents are likely to be shared widely, in the office and on social media.

In a similar case, at a bank, system conversions were also the culprit. This incident was discovered after the transfer to a new system. The IT professionals who conducted the conversion had thought it unnecessary to distinguish between personal loans and other forms of credit. The bank's management had a very different idea about what should have happened, and, when faced with the situation following the conversion, they were at their wits' end.

These examples are just a few of the numerous incidences of bad data having a detrimental effect. Think of web shops with wrongly priced goods; insurance companies that have no email addresses for the majority of their customers; banks who, when faced with specific enquiries from supervising bodies, need to mobilize a team of consultants in order to respond properly; or multinationals who have no real insight into the sales figures of some of their customers, as their subsidiaries in the various countries all use different methods of entering accounts into their systems. The promise of a comprehensive overview per customer – the so-called single version of the truth – in practice, appears to be just that: a promise.

### Inadequate data is a costly joke

According to an article in the *Harvard Business Review* in 2012,[38] every 1% of bad data causes a 10% rise in costs. A few years after that, *HBR* published an analysis[39] based on information from IBM which concluded that, in the United States alone, bad data was responsible for US$3 trillion in annual costs. In 2018, research company Gartner estimated the average annual costs of bad data per organization at US$15 million.[40] [41]

There is a world of difference between these examples and how Formula 1 racing teams deal with data (Chapter 4). The racing teams are very proud of how they use data to continuously improve their performance. All team members are aware of the importance of this data in the competition and thus they all know how vitally important high-quality data is – precisely, because it provides the very insights needed at crucial moments in the race, making the difference between win and lose. For them, it is a way of life.

## Workarounds

In many cases, data quality in organizations is poor. This often becomes clear when data-related applications leave the drawing board to be put into practice. No matter how good the algorithms are, if the fuel (i.e. the data) is inferior, the results will be too. Although companies are aware of the serious problem here, they tend to solve the matter by setting up data quality projects in which large teams work on quality improvement. In practice, this comes down to repair work and workarounds, rather than delivering any structural improvement. Data quality will only improve if everyone is convinced that winning or losing depends on that data. In Formula 1, such awareness is high and the entire team is thirsting for good and reliable data. In the business world, executives themselves often struggle to understand the importance of reliable data, never mind having to explain it to the rest of the organization.

### Data governance is relevant for all companies

Furthermore, there may be managers and directors who think data governance is only vitally relevant for data giants such as the Alibaba platform that, with over half a billion customers, is in the Champions League of data. But they would be wrong. The relationship between success and data governance applies to smaller companies as well. In an interview, Harm-Jan Stoter (top executive at Intergamma, a Dutch do-it-yourself chain) pointed to the possibilities for Intergamma's do-it-yourself stores, Karwei and Gamma, in using data to address customers in a more personalized approach.[42] As a simple yet powerful example, he takes a customer who buys a can of paint online. 'On the webpage, we then also suggest any additional relevant purchases, such as certain brushes or tape. In the past, we had to come up with the additional products ourselves, but nowadays we use a database to present these suggestions.'

It is only a minor example, but it gives an idea of why data quality is important: simply put, it fills shopping baskets.

A similar type of reasoning would apply to almost any type of business.

### Moving from FUD to strategic weaponry

The transformation that is needed in the approach to data governance shows a certain analogy with the rise of cybersecurity. Initially, organizations were driven by a fear of hackers, with businesses reacting particularly to stories in the media about the damage hackers were causing. Certain market parties anticipated this situation by applying the so-called FUD approach; they spread Fear, Uncertainty, and Doubt, which successfully struck a nerve with management boards. However, this negative, fear-driven approach often did not lead to well-thought-out security – particularly because the line of reasoning mostly had no bearing on company strategy, i.e. did not consider what most needed to be protected: the company's crown jewels. In a metaphorical sense, they were strengthening the dykes without knowing what exactly needed to be protected on the other side.

Luckily things are different now, a decade later. Cybersecurity at many organizations has become far less driven by incidents and has become SOP (standard operating procedure). Cyber risks are primarily being addressed via a risk management approach. This means that organizations focus on protecting the crown jewels rather than reacting to the perceived exterior threat. And another, at least as important, element is that cybersecurity is becoming a way for companies to strategically distinguish themselves from their competitors.

A similar development is needed with respect to data quality, which – contrary to popular belief -definitely is also a strategic competitive weapon. Which is why it should be positioned as such.

As in many other cases, here too, the sixty-four-thousand-dollar question is: How? In this situation, as in many others, there is no silver bullet. Roughly two things are needed, and for both of them the CFO could play an important role.

First of all, the CFO should be a master of persuasion to sell the importance of data quality to the whole organization.

Second, the CFO should be the architect of roles and responsibilities when it comes to data quality.

We will now dig a bit deeper into those two roles.

### Mastering the art of persuasion

It is essential that organizations are truly convinced that good data is the key to success. They need to be persuaded that, to make the best decisions and thus beat the competition, they have to be the best at using all the abundantly available information. It is just about everyday practice in Formula 1, with team leaders and managers explicitly conveying this message. It is something that is also needed to become a Decision Oriented Organization.

This belief should not be driven solely by the fact that bad data may lead to costly incidents and increased operational costs, as this effect is dwarfed by that of the opportunities that are missed if data is unreliable. In such cases, for example, new product innovations cannot be started, reliable personalized offers cannot be made, or dynamic pricing cannot be applied. It is a company's rationale; if data cannot be relied on, managers are inclined not to use them in their decision-making processes. This lack of reliable data, in effect, completely paralyses an organization.

CFOs should take the lead in communicating much more forcefully and clearly about these whys and wherefores of data governance. It may in some organizations be a somewhat thankless job. Those only looking for praise and recognition are better off focussing their efforts on developing applications for the Internet of Things, Artificial Intelligence, or Robotic Process Automation rather than trying to present a solid approach to improving data quality. Data governance is not yet a very sexy subject. The professionals who are addressing these issues, however, are in fact the ones doing the heavy lifting. They are the ones that enable others to shine. Theirs is an important role, but not one that draws major media attention or gets them tv interviews.

Data governance, in fact, struggles with perception issues – and it is up to the CFO to fix that situation. Data governance is not an obligatory element just to make sure errors are avoided – it is the key to business success and a prerequisite for seizing digital opportunities.

CFOs, therefore, must be skilled in producing clear analyses and in formulating the value of good data. In addition, they must be strongly persuasive and able to successfully convince the organization of this value – in short, they need to master the Art of Persuasion.

### Can infonomics be a driver of data quality?

One of the best ways to convince managers is to translate the importance of data governance into financial value as many managers are interested in knowing the figures. After all, as 1950s management guru Peter Drucker famously said, 'What gets measured gets done'.[43] The idea of putting a value on it is gaining traction here and there. Towards the end of the last century, Doug Laney – at the time, an analyst for Gartner's predecessor – coined the term *Infonomics*. Basically, this refers to quantifying the value of information and how to manage it as an asset. In his view, this then would lead to better decision-making, which is perfectly aligned with the central message of how to build a Decision Oriented Organization: dealing with information better leads to better decision-making, and thus to outwitting the competition. Laney also wrote a book about this subject,[44] which received relatively little attention. Unjustly so, because, now more than ever, the value of information needs to receive the appropriate amount of attention. It is the quintessence of success. Seducing organizations by providing them with financial insight into the value of data may help to increase the amount of attention they are currently awarding data governance.

## Operationalize data ownership

The second important task on the shoulders of the CFO defining roles and responsibilities.

Ownership and responsibility need to be clearly defined, including the responsibility for monitoring. This, however, should not lead to organizations setting up yet another separate department, as data governance calls for an integrated approach to joint responsibility. In practice, we see quite a few chief data officers (CDOs) appearing on the scene, with accompanying teams, to take on this task. In itself, this focused approach need not be a bad thing, as long as the responsibility for data governance is companywide.

It should be noted that CFOs have a great deal of experience with these types of challenges, albeit in a different domain. In managing and controlling financial information flows, many organizations work according to the 'three lines of defence' model. Explaining this model in detail, here, would be going too far, but a clear division of responsibilities is very important. The first line of defence – the professionals and managers running the business – governs on the basis of strategy and is therefore also responsible for information processes. The second line consists of departments with a facilitating role, for example in the areas of planning & control, risk management, process control, and data processing. They commonly also monitor the measures in the first line. The third line – the internal audit – supervises the entire process.

This model in itself has little to do with data governance, but it offers valuable lessons that may be of use in improving data governance, especially because it helps organizations to be aware of responsibilities and have the right mindset. If this model works as it should,[45] the responsibility for reliable financial information is understood throughout the organization. This model could be applied in a wider sense to also include data governance, for which it would be essential that the first line fully acknowledges its responsibilities.

This is not an automatic process and, as already mentioned, means that a customer service department, for example, must not only be run to focus on efficiency and quality, but, in its contact with customers, also be tasked with checking customer information against the company's database. This implies that workflows ensure data quality, which could be achieved by implementing the right type of software. After all, data quality can at least partly be attained by design in work flows. These are typically aspects on which the second line would be best suited to provide advice and facilitate implementation.

### Facing a dilemma

Many organizations are faced with the chicken-or-the-egg dilemma. Often in business, people are not very worried about data quality, as they see only a few useful applications of data-driven technology yet and do not grasp the related opportunities. Anything that does not contribute directly to return on investment faces the chopping block. However, application developers are pleading for higher data quality, as this would give them the opportunity to show what they can do and, thus, increase the ROI in the long run.

Breaking this stalemate calls for leadership. True leaders are also able to play the long game when it comes to earning potential, apart from focusing on quarterly figures. Reliable data is becoming an increasingly important driver of that earning potential. And so, it is high time for this story to be told, in no uncertain terms. Sounds like a nice job for CFOs.

## Core messages to CFOs:

✓ **Position Data Governance as an organization-wide responsibility**
Data quality can only be more sustainably improved if it becomes an organization-wide responsibility. This is why clearly defining responsibilities is so important. Data quality could be facilitated by a data governance department to lead the organization in the right direction, but it should never take over this responsibility from the rest of the organization.

✓ **Clearly explain the opportunities that would be created once data governance has been taken to a higher level**
Data governance is the key to success in an era of digital transformation, offering many new opportunities and creating customer value. It is of the highest strategic importance and is much more than a somewhat boring compliance topic. The more clearly those opportunities are formulated and communicated, the more enthusiasm they would generate.

✓ **Provide insight into the financial value of data**
Measure to Manage. Many managers need facts and figures to lead their organization. Those capable of expressing the value of data in such facts and figures will also be able to increase the focus on data quality.

## 6.2   Make sure you understand the story behind the data

*Digital technology helps us make better decisions and often greatly increases predictability. CFOs also have the job of spurring this on, as we argue in this book. Because missing this wave of new opportunities also means being defeated by the competition.*

*Be that as it may, we also need to add some reservations to this optimistic stance. Being hungry for the opportunities related to data is fine, but data analysis and/or Artificial Intelligence should not be applied haphazardly and unquestioningly, without an eye for possible failures or mistakes. It is important to understand what you are doing, more than anything else. More to the point, organizations must remain vigilant and ensure that the use of data does not lead to nonsensical decisions.*

*Again, CFOs are ideally equipped to handle this. Together with their teams, they can push back against overenthusiastic data scientists who may be blinded by mathematics, lead technological applications into the right direction, and thus avoid many disappointments. CFOs should be the critical conscience when it comes to the use of data analysis and do everything in their power to recognize and properly interpret phenomena and patterns that emerge from that data, based on their contextual knowledge of the business. With better questions, they can make sure that the machine provides better answers.*

In 2008, Chris Anderson, chief editor of the influential US technology magazine *Wired*, wrote an article with a rather bold title: 'The end of theory: the data deluge makes the scientific method obsolete'.[46]

Anderson postulated the idea that, in a world with just about all conceivable data and almost infinite computing power, we no longer need scientific explanations for any phenomena. And we owe this progress to the clever minds in Silicon Valley who, from now on, will show us the way by capturing the whole world in data. An important element of Anderson's argument is a quote from one of those clever minds, Peter Norvig, director of Google's research department. He is said to have stated at a conference: 'All models are wrong, and increasingly you can succeed without them.' Anderson concludes: 'Correlation supersedes causation, and science can advance even without coherent models, unified theories, or really any mechanistic explanation at all.'

**Was that a silly statement?**
That is quite a statement; according to Anderson, there is no need for us to understand why anything happens now that we can capture reality in data with surgical precision. At the time, the article was a true sign of the times, of how optimism about data can go overboard. A small but not insignificant detail is Norvig himself claiming his statement was completely misrepresented. As he says on his own website: 'That's a silly statement, I didn't say it, and I disagree with it'.[47] On his site he also claims that Anderson later confessed to him that the story in *Wired* was mainly meant to throw a stone in the pond and provoke some discussion. *You shouldn't check a good story to death*, an old journalist joke says....

More than a decade on, spurred by Silicon Valley people, Artificial Intelligence has become quite the rage among policymakers and administrators. Real-time data is increasingly used for making on-the-spot decisions which is quite a contrast to how we used to rely on traditional econometric models. At the same time, however, we realize all too well that scientific models still have their purpose and it is a good thing that we have not thrown that baby out with the bathwater just yet in favour of AI applications. Although scientific models have their limitations – to quote George Box, a well-known statistician, 'all models are wrong but some are useful '- Silicon Valley solutions quite regularly also tend to perform less well than expected.

### Is that a tabby cat or is it a bowl of guacamole?

An example of the status of AI is how Google's image recognition system, InceptionV3, can cleverly be manipulated into asserting that a perfectly good photograph of a tabby cat is actually one of a bowl of guacamole.[48] An equally entertaining case is that of a former MIT director and a group of students in the United States who developed the 'Basic Automatic B.S.[49] Essay Language (BABEL) Generator, a program that patched together strings of sophisticated words and sentences into meaningless essays. The nonsense essays consistently received high, sometimes perfect, scores when run through different scoring programs.' They found that the automated scoring engines often used for grading student essays could easily be fooled, as the tooling rewarded the essays with high scores and concluded that the essays which were cobbled together by machines each represented a 'competent examination of the argument and convey(ed) meaning with acceptable clarity'.[50]

### Can excel errors change history?

Technology can go utterly and completely wrong if we are insufficiently critical of how it is used. And that goes far beyond a few funny examples. The immaturity of Artificial Intelligence and data analysis is demonstrated almost every week somewhere in the media, in all conceivable areas. A glaring example is that of the 2016 American general elections, when the analytical tools of almost all forecasters predicted a comfortable win for Hillary Clinton, after which her opponent, Donald Trump, went on to win the presidency. This led to enormous debate about opinion polls and the underlying data collection methods.

Even if the underlying data is reliable and properly collected, things can go badly wrong. The analytic model may be flawed. Sometimes it may even be as basic as a mishap in an Excel sheet. In 2010, two prominent American economists published a paper[51] in which they warned that US debt was getting out of hand and becoming a threat to the economy. After intense political debate about the pros and cons of austerity, it became evident that they had made a simple mistake in their Excel model which overstated the effect of high debt on the economy. Bloomberg online later published an explanation, with a bold title: the 'Excel Error That Changed History'.[52]

Or, a little closer to home for CFOs: for a number of years, Aegon USA Investment Management worked with quantitative investment models developed by one of their junior analysts to provide asset management advice to investors. These models proved to contain numerous errors. It was not until this was made public that Aegon decided to formulate validation procedures for such models. In 2019, the United States Securities and Exchange Commission (SEC) fined Aegon US$97 million.[53] A somewhat similar case refers to a message from BlackRock, the world's largest investment manager. On closer inspection, its management decided to shelve two promising

AI models on estimating liquidity risk because they were unable to explain the models. Their argument against deployment of the models read. 'The senior people want to see something they can understand'.[54]

The latter makes an essential point. With respect to the use of algorithms, many experts consider explicability an important prerequisite. If we are unable to explain or understand how an algorithm arrives at its conclusions, the prudent thing to do is to give it a wide berth. This sounds sensible, and is also reminiscent of how the 2007-2008 credit crisis first started – many bank executives were forced to admit that they themselves did not understand some of their financial products at all.

However, healthy vigilance in this area should not morph into overly rigid attitudes, as this may block progress altogether. For example, major dilemmas may arise in situations where data patterns offer physicians life-saving advice on treatment, but those physicians – because of the limitations of the human brain to deal with great complexity – are unable to understand *why* the advice is so useful.

**Premature baby**
This situation is far from inconceivable, as demonstrated at a Canadian hospital where babies born prematurely were treated on the basis on Artificial Intelligence. Infections are among the greatest risks to babies in incubators. At the Toronto hospital, researchers were able to detect patterns in the data that predict such infections before the child shows any signs of illness, up to 24 hours in advance. This would enable medical staff to anticipate the health problem. Why the pattern occurred could not be explained by the medical specialists, at

least at that time. There was a clear correlation without any explanation of causality.[55]

The limits to the explicability of data analysis are also starting to play a role outside the medical world. For example, in a paper[56] on the future of auditors using Artificial Intelligence for their annual auditing reports, the American Institute of Certified Public Accountants (AICPA) wrote: 'simply knowing that something is likely to occur is more important than understanding exactly the reason. It is analogous to auditing applications in which restatements, accounting fraud, bankruptcy, or going-concern issues are correlated with indicators obtained from company filings and sources of data.'

**No miracle cure**
In other words, the fact that we cannot understand exactly why something happens is beside the point. In accountancy, there are no lives at stake and the paper's authors have chosen an all too easy line of reasoning that is typical of our time. The way new digital technology is trusted, sometimes, knows no limits and it seems to be the silver bullet, the solution for solving any and all problems. Merely adding Artificial Intelligence to a project has a magical effect, even when below the surface there is no intelligence of any kind involved.

Optimism is a good thing, as long as realists are also involved to step on the brakes now and then, to ensure that such Artificial Intelligence does not turn into *Artificial Unintelligence.*[57] Because it is precisely the abundance of data and computing power that is creating the enormous risk of recognizing patterns that occur purely coincidentally and, therefore, serve no purpose at all.

CFOs therefore need to be the critical conscience when deploying digital technology and do everything in their power to continue to explain the phenomena and patterns that arise from data. The fact that the complexity of the matter imposes limits on what they can do does not mean they should not try.

To carve out the CFO's role, two interrelated issues are important, which are elaborated in more detail below.

First, there is the question of whether the applications are indeed using the most relevant data.

The second question is whether outcomes make sense based on the context.

**Check not only whether the data is right but also whether it is the right data**
Data reliability and integrity are of course important to arrive at well-founded decisions, as we argued in Section 6.1 on Data Governance. But reliable data by itself does not make for sound decisions – a model is as good as the data you put into it, and the right decision may perhaps require completely different data than that used in a particular model.

An effective illustration of how this works is demonstrated by talent management within an organization. From attracting the best talent on the labour market to management development policies, more and more organizations choose to act by using data analysis, the idea being that technology helps to identify top talent characteristics to watch out for, and can subsequently be used to predict which new candidates have the best chance of becoming such top talent. This type of technology, thus, aids management in making better decisions on human resources and company programmes for its high potentials.

The key question, here, relates to determining what data would be the most relevant. Quite understandably, the university attended and final grades at that university are regarded as important variables. This can nevertheless be extremely misleading. Consider the fact that people may have graduated cum laude from a top university because they are exceptionally clever. However, it could also be that they grew up in a wealthy environment with parents who knew the right people to get their child into that top university and who spent loads of money on private tuition in order to boost the grades on the final list. The latter type of candidate may do well in the organization, but that does not exclude the possibility of an even better candidate out there somewhere. Finding these other candidates requires other variables. The examples on this subject are numerous, and, in recent years, the debate has included the closely related discrimination by algorithms.

This principle is an issue that arises with any application of data analysis and Artificial Intelligence (and, in fact, also in management information in general, see text box). Fraud detection is a subject that is a little closer to the CFO's environment. Data containing all the characteristics of past incidences of fraud can very easily be fed into a model and are likely to also greatly strengthen the safety net for identifying future fraud cases. However, it is debatable whether those variables are truly the most relevant ones and whether their application provides the best picture, or if perhaps this reveals only the tip of the iceberg, leaving most information in the dark uncertainty of the deep blue sea.[58]

### Beware of misleading metrics

Management information is the instrument of choice with which to keep a finger on the pulse of strategy implementation (performance management). If the indicators – the metrics – suit that strategy, managers have a great instrument for comparing strategic plans to real output.

This is all in theory, of course. In reality, things can often go wrong because the indicators have drifted away from the implementation of the strategy. In such cases, they measure something completely different, and this carries enormous risks. People tend to focus on optimizing the indicator ('metrics fixation') without applying any common sense to wonder whether the underlying strategic goal is really being served.

A rather painful example is that of American bank Wells Fargo, where, in 2016, employees overenthusiastically set to work to push customers into taking out new credit cards. According to many, the incident was a cross-selling strategy that had gone off the rails. Over the course of that year, Wells Fargo issued no fewer than 3.5 million new credit cards to customers, even to those who had not agreed to it. In the end, for the bank, this led to hundreds of millions of dollars in fines and lawsuits. It also generated a lot of bad publicity. An analysis in the *Harvard Business Review* pointed to the weak spot: 'The real source of Wells Fargo's problems was measurement. When the bank decided to actively track daily cross-sales numbers, employees rationally responded by working to maximise them. Throw in financial incentives, a permissive culture, and intense demands placed on performance, and they might even illegally open some unauthorised accounts, all in the name of advancing the "strategy" of cross-selling.'[59]

The most salient aspect, from our story's perspective, is that the same analysis afterwards showed that Wells Fargo did not even have a cross-selling strategy at all! It only used an indicator in its management information system to put the emphasis on cross-selling. A painful example, therefore, of an unsuitable indicator.

Using indicators is a good idea. After all, managers must have some tangible instrument through which they can understand the environment, results, and objectives and translate those into what employees should be doing. But, as the Wells Fargo case illustrates so well, it is essential to align indicators with the actual strategy. Not doing so poses enormous risk.

### Critically question data background

In the 1980s and 1990s, New York City was dealing with a significant crime wave. Its police commissioner at the time, William Bratton, looked for ways to address this problem and he did so on the basis of the 1982 'broken windows theory',[60] which states that small offences grow into serious crimes if not dealt with in time. Precisely for this reason, New York City developed a zero-tolerance policy and increased the number of police officers patrolling the streets.

The result: the number of crimes soon diminished and security in New York City improved enormously. Many studies directly linked this improvement to the policies of hardliner Mayor Rudi Giuliani, who, at the time, was put on a pedestal as the great crimefighter who made New York City safe again.

But there is also another side to this story, as recorded in the book *Freakonomics*.[61] Researchers discovered that crime decreased in regions where abortion had been legalized twenty years earlier. The causal relationship appeared to be that if poor mothers were all given the opportunity to terminate their pregnancy, this would prevent the next vulnerable group of people from being born. In a certain number of years after that, it is inevitable that the crime rate would take a nose dive. Which is what happened in New York City.

Having a critical attitude with regard to the distinction between correlation and causality is of growing importance in a world in which we rely on data. This distinction is sometimes difficult to make though.

The belief that data does not produce 'objective' or 'hard' truths is becoming more widespread. Good data scientists (and, more generally, digital application developers) are aware of such risks. They are familiar with the so-called Simpson's Paradox. One example known to statisticians is the medical treatment of kidney stones. Treatment method A is a normal operation, method B is based on a small incision. Overall, the statistics of the treatments show that treatment B is the best for the patient. But a completely different picture emerges when we divide the group of patients into those with small kidney stones and those with large kidney stones. Treatment

A then turns out to be the best option for both groups. What may have seemed illogical at first glance can be explained when taking these things into account. Although CFOs and controllers do not need to know the exact background of this Simpson's Paradox,[62] they must realize that the answer to the often-heard question of 'What does the data tell us?' is not always the most obvious one.

As mentioned before, good data scientists do realize there are pitfalls in interpreting data, which is why they appreciate the importance of contextual knowledge. Therefore, as a control mechanism, CFOs could ask them in passing whether they have heard of Simpson's Paradox. Should that result in a glassy eyed look, that would definitely be a red flag.

### Explore the story behind the data

Such knowledge is only one of the things that may be expected from a professional department involved in developing data analysis and AI. There is yet another analogy with the rise of the Internet. In the 1990s, every company wished to have its own website, and there was always a proverbial handyman available to make that wish come true.

Now, a few decades later, there is enormous professionalisation in organizations implementing online strategies. Something similar is happening with regard to algorithm development. Many organizations have enthusiastically started to address these subjects, and, while doing so, are understanding that certain things should be professionalized. In practice, however, this type of professionalism is still a long way off and, sometimes, resembles well-intentioned amateurism. To prevent nonsensical conclusions from being drawn, it is particularly important for data to be regarded in combination with context, rather than purely from a statistical perspective. This is why successful data analysis always consists of collaboration between those knowledgeable about the subject matter on the one hand and data scientists on the other.

Generally speaking, it is always a good idea to look for the story behind the data. The story provides relevance. And this, again, is ideally something that CFOs could take on, in the first place, because CFOs, in their role of financial expert in a broad sense, are busy every day interpreting information, often with knowledge of the business context. But at least as important is the fact that CFOs also have lots of experience in poking holes in overly optimistic business cases. Their professionally critical attitude enables them to get to the heart of the matter and, if necessary, mercilessly take apart any slick scenario. This experience also comes in handy to ensure that, in other areas as well, their organization's management is not fooled by data analysis and will not look for conclusions that fit the context.

An illustrative example: an insurance company discovered that anyone who regularly buys fresh fennel at a supermarket is less likely to claim on their insurance. The explanation being that this person is probably a home cook and 'home cooks were less likely to claim on their insurance and therefore are more profitable. It's a finding that makes good intuitive sense. There probably isn't much crossover between the group of people who are willing to invest time, effort, and money into creating an elaborate dish from scratch and the group who would let their children play football in the house'.[63] Nothing to do with the fennel itself per se. The data only makes sense when you know the context.

### Process mining: only in context

Making sense of data almost always requires a certain amount of knowledge of the context from which that data originates. This can also be seen in process mining. In essence, this means that every activity leaves a digital trail – from approving an invoice for payment to receiving a parcel in the post, adjusting a price, and entering a car park. With process mining, maps of processes can be created with surgical precision, and numerous exceptions and striking patterns can be discerned in the data.

This can be very useful for detecting fraud, mapping desire paths inside organizations, changing certain function divisions, and exposing inefficient processes. Working with such a tool may lead to many questions. Why are certain deliveries always delayed? How are some employees able to apply workarounds to the calibrated procedures? Number crunching will not automatically result in valuable information in those cases, though; only if the data is considered with contextual knowledge of the processes – and their associated employees, suppliers, or customers – can questions be asked and answered in a way that will make sense. Or, in the words of Dutch professor Wil van der Aalst, one of the initiators in the field of process mining: 'It is the process *and* the data, stupid'.[64]

At Amazon, one of the companies operating in the so-called Champions League of data and algorithms, they are aware of the importance of context. Top executive Jeff Bezos, especially, aims to go beyond the data and expects people who are attending his meetings to spend the first half hour reading a memorandum of up to six pages that explains the purpose of the meeting. The basic principle here being that managers can present their proposals in the form of a story that is told in such a way that everyone will be able to understand it. It is quite remarkable that even in a distinctly data-driven organization such as Amazon, the 'story' is considered so important. Bezos said about this in an explanation: 'The thing I noticed is that when the anecdotes and the data disagree, the anecdotes are usually right. There's something wrong with the way you're measuring'.[65]

### If you want better answers, start with better questions

This chapter is not intended as an argument against data-driven decisions. However, throwing as much data as possible at a problem is often meaningless. Data by itself does not usually produce any ideas; at best, all it does is refine, explore, or test ideas. This chapter, therefore, is primarily about understanding the limits to what data and the associated concepts can do. Knowing what data could be used for can only be understood once the constraints are known. CFOs and their teams are to monitor and protect those boundaries, asking critical questions and applying analytical skills. After all, this is exactly what CFOs and controllers have always done with financial information: looking for the causal relationships – how value is created – and getting at the story behind the figures. If we expect better answers from data, humans simply have to ask better questions.

## Core messages to CFOs:

✓ **Assess developers' degree of professionality**
Professional development of data analysis and/or Artificial Intelligence calls for more than just the smartest minds; it also requires an environment in which there is professional collaboration with subject matter experts. Because number crunching without context is extremely dangerous.

✓ **Explore the story behind the data**
Data can be either a rich source of insight or be highly misleading. Patterns and conclusions based on data sets should therefore be studied closely by people who truly understand the particular context. This knowledge can then be used to decide why those patterns occur and why the conclusions are either justified or not, greatly reducing the risk of useless or even disastrous application of data and mitigating the risk of tunnel vision.

✓ **Aim for data analyses that you can explain**
If the way an algorithm works can no longer be unambiguously explained to non-specialists (especially to top management), the risks are twofold: wrong conclusions may be drawn, or conclusions may be right but will not be accepted. Although explainability has its limits when it comes to Artificial Intelligence, one should at least give it a shot.

## 6.3 Don't be afraid to standardize

*Bakeries are different from, say, cement factories. So, obviously, they should be supported by the most suitable, appropriate systems. They deserve tailor-made systems.*

*Do they? Or is it more complicated than that?*

*Particularly in the case of so-called enterprise resource planning (ERP) systems, aiming for tailor-made systems often leads to disappointing results. There are two reasons to consider.*

*In the first place, expectations about how ERP systems can be differentiators are too high. Such systems themselves do not lead to success, but rather are intended to be the reliable backbone of operations.*

*This has everything to do with the second point. As many organizations are afraid to standardize their work processes and data, they create unnecessary complexity when implementing ERP systems. This is a serious issue, as it causes information processing to be far from optimal, and is a threat to a company's competitive position.*

*The core message: Organizations are less distinctive than their managers tend to believe. Processes, products, and organizations require a greater level of standardization. At first glance, this sounds boring, obstructive, customer-unfriendly, and stifling for creativity. But looking at it from a certain distance provides a completely different picture, one in which increased standardization actually reduces complexity and provides rather than stifles the essential breeding ground for creative and innovative applications.*

For seven years, German supermarket chain Lidl worked on the implementation of the ERP system known as SAP (Systems, Applications & Products in data processing). The exact investment level has so far not been made public but is estimated to run into the hundreds of millions of euros, according to an analysis by German newspaper *Handelsblatt*.[66] Over time, however, the project, named eLWIS (pronounced as 'Elvis' in German), proved less flexible in the hips than its namesake. In 2018, management pulled the plug on the project.

*Handelsblatt*'s analysis revealed that Lidl was looking for a tailor-made implementation. For example, they adapted the system to include stocks at cost prices while the rest of the industry uses retail prices. Such adjustments are risky, because 'altering existing software is like changing a prefab house; you can put the kitchen cupboards in a different place, but when you start moving the walls, there's no stability'.

What does this case tell us about implementing ERP systems?

Generally speaking, managers are not very keen on implementing ERP systems – they often distrust the developers and the promises they make. The term ERP particularly evokes images of runaway projects that fail to deliver what they promise. Such situations are partly created by the organizations themselves making multiple changes to customize systems entirely to their individual wishes. In reality, ERP systems are not suitable for too much customization; processes can be integrated and automated, but trying to tweak the system in order to retain a large variety of existing working methods, processes, and definitions sets it up for failure. It would be much better to do this the other way around: i.e. using the system's implementation as the ideal opportunity to standardize working methods.

## Forms of complexity

Before we discuss this subject in more detail, we should analyse the enormous diversity a little more closely. It is a phenomenon that is directly related to the concept of organizational complexity, with a twofold distinction between *rewarded* and *unrewarded* complexity[67], as identified by Frans van Houten, CEO of Philips. The first form of complexity is part and parcel of the market in which a company operates and of the demands and expectations of its customers. It is described as 'rewarding' in the sense of the obvious financial value it creates. This makes the companies who successfully navigate this complexity stand out from the crowd.

In contrast, the second form of complexity is highly pernicious. It is incorporated into organizations without creating any value, financial or otherwise. Examples would be additional management layers, complicated reporting structures and the like.

## Rewarded complexity

To a certain extent, this distinction in the way an organization is designed can also be applied to systems design. The challenge lies in only allowing rewarded complexity and, thus, avoid adding complexity that would not enhance the company's ability to distinguish itself in the market. Simply put: adding a certain functionality to give customers insight into the real-time status of their order, for example, would in some markets be a case of rewarded complexity. Adjusting a system only because the internal organizational structure calls for it is an example of unrewarded complexity.

This is where things often go wrong. The symptoms of unrewarded complexity concerning systems include: an excessive number of change requests from within the organization; endless amounts of time in workshops to determine system parameters; a large number of changes compared to the standard configuration; and the need for many external consultants for system development and management. Once such a customization has been approved, emotion often wins over rational thought. Organizations and people, basically, believe they are unique and therefore need a unique system. But from a rational perspective, this is not the case.

**Three segments**

Processes can be divided into three segments:

- **Foundational (60%).** These are the basic processes needed for an organization to be able to function, and are mainly concerned with efficiency and low costs. Customization is often expensive and adds little or no benefit to those basic processes.
- **Competitive (30%).** The organization needs to operate at least as well as the competition. Most of the processes in this middle category are also very suitable for standardization.
- **Distinctive (10%).** This is where organizations distinguish themselves from others. The processes through which they make a difference in the market. For this category, it makes sense to strive for the best processes and to go for tailor-made solutions.

The emergence of relatively new concepts such as Cloud Platforms, Artificial Intelligence, and Robotic Process Automation leaves organizations little choice but to standardize rather ruthlessly. After all, these types of technologies are placing some of the work processes outside of the organization. Those who hold on to company-specific working methods which have often evolved historically will no longer be able to participate in such new developments. Moreover, organizations are increasingly operating within so-called ecosystems that also include other parties. The interfaces with those other parties need to run smoothly, which is why it is important to customize them as little as possible and to embrace the standards.

More standardization is the motto. There are roughly four arguments in favour of this: (1) Standardization leads to greater efficiency; (2) Standardization paves the way for new digital applications such as robots; (3) Standardization facilitates tailor-made products and services (really? yes, really); and (4) Standardization leads to more reliable information. These arguments are discussed in more detail below.

### Standardization leads to greater efficiency
Uniformity and cost saving go hand in hand, almost by definition. This is a no brainer. Uniformity in processes is simply cheaper – something that is vitally important in a digital environment with hyper-competition.

The effect of such uniformity is often even much greater than anticipated, which has everything to do with the so-called 'hidden factory'.[68] In the LEAN Six Sigma approach, the term hidden factory describes activities that usually seem to be real activities but in reality are recovery processes related to other activities; things like handling rejected goods, restoring errors, or handling complaints. Here, the risk of creating hidden factories is substantial, precisely in relation to such highly customized processes. The work done in these hidden factories is of no value whatsoever. The rule of thumb among LEAN experts is that these hidden processes account for about 30% of the costs. Certainly no small matter.

## Workarounds

All sorts of processes can have such hidden factories within them, in production environments as well as services and administrative processes. How to detect and defuse such costly workarounds is beyond the scope of this book and is more a task for experts well trained in Lean Six Sigma. But the fact that a lack of uniformity leads to enormous waste in the form of such workarounds is a lesson that we must take into account when designing systems. The good news is that awareness of this phenomenon is growing. For example, ERP systems increasingly use standard features (also called templates) in which certain functions or other parameters, such as cost centres or purchasing conditions, are already filled in.

## Standardization paves the way for new digital applications

Expectations around technological concepts such as Artificial Intelligence and Robotic Process Automation have been very promising over the past years. Nevertheless, the pace at which these concepts are conquering the world of business can still be disappointing – which is partly due to a lack of standardization of processes and systems.

The relationship between this slower-than-expected progress in those technologies and standardization is easily explained.

A robot is very good at observing and registering how people do things and can simply copy them. However, the more exceptions (i.e. desire paths) there are in a process, the greater the need for people to stay involved and/or the more is demanded of a robot's learning ability. A robot is not very good at handling desire paths, but if more processes and work routines were to take place according to a standardized approach, the real profits and benefits will come within reach.

For organizations, this is also an argument in favour of reducing the complexity of their IT environment. Meanwhile, 'smarter' robots are also being developed. Intelligent Process Automation (IPA) increases cognitive ability including how to handle desire paths. But here we see too that robots will be more effective if the basis on which they are used (including the ERP systems) is standardized.

### Standardization facilitates tailor-made products and services

Is arguing in favour of standardization not tantamount to denying the benefits of digitization in the twenty-first century? After all, we live in an era of extreme expectations. Consumers these days are only satisfied with the best of the best in terms of convenience and performance. And preferably for free. It goes even further; consumers also expect producers and service providers to anticipate their needs rather than responding to them. Which can be done, with today's technology: if a sensor on your heater can signal a malfunction, the heater is surely also able to tell you about it and ask whether it should go ahead and organize for a service engineer to come and fix the problem.

Trend watcher Steven van Belleghem summed it up perfectly: *We don't want Siri, we want Samantha.*[69] The implicit message being we do not settle for the rudimentary voice control on an iPhone; we want the empathic, almost human, service of Samantha, the digital assistant from the science fiction film *Her* by director Spike Jonze. An assistant who knows us and meets our needs according to our personal desires.

This is all calling out for custom applications. How can the plea for more standardization of processes also be true?

The answer: standardization in the underlying processes is precisely what is needed to offer customization on the output side. Or, in management terms, if you standardize the back office, having the right interfaces in the front office means you can offer tailor-made customer journeys. Hyper-relevant proposals are only possible if the information available on each customer is extremely detailed. Many of the new kids on the block understand this totally, and, therefore, implement highly standardized processes and systems in their back offices. For them, this is precisely the way to enable contextual understanding – the basis for customization.

**Standardization leads to more reliable information**
During his frequent visits to subsidiaries in other countries, the CFO of a global multinational saw a proliferation of reports and analyses by the company's local business controllers. From time to time, the figures presented in them could not be traced back to the information that was centrally available at the head office. This was an unsatisfactory situation, to say the least, because it posed the enormous risk of important decisions being based on incorrect or biased information.

In a daring move, he decided from then on to talk only about reports that could be demonstrated to have been checked beforehand and/or connected to the central systems. For the controllers at the subsidiaries, this took some getting used to, as they were losing some of their autonomy. But it also ensured that no more energy was lost in discussing whether information was correct or not. And it also turned out to be an extremely practical way of arriving at the often-heard 'single version of the truth'.

This is in line with an example from MIT scientist Jeanne Ross, who years ago advocated the use of 'data dictators'.[70] In an interview, she refers to how the top executive of insurer Aetna called all their business managers together to develop a plan to turn the insurer's heavy losses into profits. On the basis of the figures in their own reports, each of the managers claimed their unit was profitable. This was of course impossible; if all the units were making a profit, there would be no losses at all. To address this problem, the executive decided that he would determine from where the figures were to be obtained and according to which definitions. He simply enforced the 'single version of the truth' concept.

For many organizations, this concept has become an important theme. Quite understandably so, as having only one version of the truth is by no means self-evident, in a world with complex and fragmented systems. In an ideal world, everyone works with the same information and the same definitions. In reality things are very different, certainly in organizations that have a wide variety of systems, for example, as a result of merger or takeovers. This is another reason why standardization is useful: it puts an end to much of the confusion about information, and people's attention can be focused on making the best decisions instead of on sorting through definitions and sources of information. This is even more true when organizations want to optimize processes across their value chain in a joint effort with their suppliers and customers.

### Ergo: more standardization, please

Smart executives protect their organizations against excessive customization. This applies to the implementation of ERP systems, among other things, as described at the beginning of this chapter. In recent years, vendors offer more and more excellent best practice solutions for this purpose, which are in fact a form of standardization. Managers should at least give these best practices a fair chance. A Gartner[71] guide contains a simple and ironic decision tree for weighing up best practices. After an initial assessment (about whether a unique process leads to value), question 2 reads: 'Willing to change business process to pre-defined process?' If the answer is no, Gartner 'allows' you to opt for customization, but this should really put you in an automatic feedback loop to bring you to the question: 'Are you sure you're not willing to change?'

In practice, few people are brave enough to opt for standardization. Although this fear is unjustified, because, as Gartner says (and is also mentioned earlier in this chapter), 'By definition, best-practice processes alone cannot lead to value. But they can underpin differentiation or innovation. Their value is in standardised and repeated use of formalised and predictable business processes. They can support an organization's competitive advantage and provide an opportunity to achieve gains by converting inefficient activities into streamlined, structured processes.'

A vanguard of organizations focus on standardization, not only in IT systems but also in organizational structures. Many larger companies have been working on such transformations for many years, often under the common mantra of 'One Company'. They recognize that this standardization lays the foundation for more speed and flexibility which is essential in the current era of digital transformation.

Ross & Weill[72] offer an excellent theoretical background in their book on Enterprise Architecture. Their book describes a quadrant of four different operating models. Along the y-axis, the degree of process integration, and the x-axis showing the degree of standardization. Thus, four types of models emerge:

1. Diversification (low standardization, low integration): 'independence with shared service.'
2. Coordination (low standardization, high integration): 'seamless access to shared data'
3. Replication (high standardization, low integration): 'standardized independence'
4. Unification (high standardization, high integration) 'standardized, integrated processes'

According to the authors, what matters is that management determine which type of operating model would best suit the typology of their organization and its external context (the market). For the very reason that, as we said earlier, a bakery is not a cement factory.

To decide on the degree of uniformity, only two questions are really important: (1) To what extent is the success of an organizational unit dependent on the availability, reliability, and speed of data from another business? And (2) how much does one unit benefit from the fact that another unit operates in the same way?

Especially now that we are in the midst of a digital transformation, the answer to these questions will increasingly and uncompromisingly point to type 4: Unification. The philosophy being that the organization is regarded as a single entity with far-reaching standardization of processes and systems. As the authors themselves say: 'When organizational units are tightly integrated around a standardized set of processes, companies benefit from a Unification model. Companies applying this model find little benefit in business unit autonomy. They maximise efficiencies and customer services by presenting integrated data and driving variability out of business processes.'

Unsurprisingly, many organizations recognize and want to take advantage of the blessings of standardization, especially when it comes to non-primary processes such as Finance, HR, IT, and procurement. They also want to do away with IT 'spaghetti' systems. The Ross & Weill model could eliminate much of the previously described 'unrewarded complexity'. Tackling this issue as if it were purely an IT issue, however, would be one of the pitfalls. In reality, addressing it would start with a complete organizational transformation followed by the standardization of IT as a logical consequence. And patently not the other way around.

## Core messages to CFOs:

✓ **Critically analyse which complexities we could do without**

Complex and/or diverse processes or systems are some-times needed to create value for customers. Certain forms of complexity, however, do not add any value. They need to be reduced as quickly as possible.

✓ **Force everybody to talk about the same information**

As long as not everyone is talking about the same facts and figures, most of the energy will go into discussing the data. Enforcing a 'single version of the truth' would bring the dis-cussion's focus back to content. Standardization will help to achieve this.

✓ **Tell a convincing story about the advantages of standardization**

Standardization of processes and systems offers enormous opportunities for the deployment of new technology and im-proves anticipation of the needs of customers. To convince people, however, a convincing narrative is needed about these benefits.

**In closing...**

In this chapter we argued that CFOs have three main tasks in preparing their organizations for a world in which decisions are made entirely differently: Properly organizing data governance; maintaining a critical attitude towards the conclusions that data analysis produces; and more standardization of information systems. In themselves, the three tasks already form a challenging combination, but they are merely the basis for transforming into a Decision Oriented Organization. Much more is needed. The following chapter discusses all the tasks CFOs are faced with if they are to drastically improve decision-making on essential issues.

# Chapter 7  Decision-making

FROM
going with the flow
TO
the art of looking sideways

*The way we make decisions will change thoroughly, as we argue in this book. And, from our point of view, chief financial officers (CFOs) should be tasked with pushing this process in the right direction. This not only requires sound data, good systems, and good algorithms (roughly the subject of Chapter 6), but also calls for fundamentally altering decision-making processes, in line with the modus operandi at Formula 1 teams. It means that other types of information must also be taken into account to live up to the promise of forward-looking analysis; it means that human 'herd animal' errors are to be suppressed; and it calls for a whole new cooperation between humans and smart machines. How could these three major issues be addressed?*

In 2009, Ukrainian Jan Koum, while taking a break after being turned down for a job at Facebook, bought his first iPhone. Apple had just launched the concept of the Appstore and together with his friend Brian Acton, Koum saw possibilities for offering a new messaging service through that platform. He called his product WhatsApp, derived from the expression 'what's up'. In the first few months after the app's launch, there were technical problems and the app was downloaded only a limited number of times, but after a while its use started to take more serious form and, before long, mushroomed into exponential growth in the number of users.

Some clever analysts in the telecom industry soon realized that this was going to completely change the revenue model of telecom companies. At that time, the CEOs of those telecom companies were mainly presented with graphs showing the lucrative income growth from SMS traffic. Even if there had been analysts brave enough to stand up and tell them about this new concept and how, soon, their beautiful growth curve of SMS revenues was likely to change, at best they would have been dismissed with a friendly 'thanks for presenting your insights'.

In 2014, five years after its conception, WhatsApp had over 500 million active users and SMS revenues were down to virtually nothing. Marc Zuckerberg invited Koum to dinner and a few weeks later announced that Facebook was buying the company for about US$20 billion. By late 2017, the app had 1.5 billion active monthly users.

This case says a lot about successful entrepreneurship.

First of all, the case shows once again that relevance is the starting point, as we argued in Chapter 3. Success is not primarily attained through a clever revenue model; success starts with products or services that people value. This is wonderfully illustrated in a tweet by Koum in which he warned: 'Next person to call me an entrepreneur is getting punched in the face by my bodyguard. Seriously'.[73] Koum saw money mainly as a means to an end. All he wanted to do was make great stuff. More important to this chapter is the second point, namely that not all important insights can be derived from conventional management reports. Anyone who wants to be successful in business needs to be able to anticipate the future, recognizing new and upcoming developments, and assess their likely impact on the organization's strategy. But this is not only done by analysing the financials of recent months, nor by getting a rolling forecast for the coming months, but also by collecting very different information, and data analytics can make a major contribution to this. Hence the title of this chapter: *From going with the flow to the art of looking sideways.*

Finally, the WhatsApp case also teaches us that being successful often means not making the same – in this case technological – choices that the rest of the industry has been making. Above all, executives and managers must make an independent assessment on the basis of the right information.

These are all matters in which CFOs can and must play a central role. This chapter examines how. Here is our call to CFOs:

**Look beyond the financial data** (7.1)
Companies should not be fixated on management information obtained from general ledger systems because these often do not hold the information that really matters and that offers forward-looking potential. CFOs, therefore, should step out of their comfort zone and reinvent management information (and/or how decisions are made) based on a mix of data. Financial and non-financial. Internal and external. Traditional financial information only plays a minor role in this respect.

## Don't be a penguin (7.2)

Humans have a strong tendency to copy each other's behaviour and opinions. This is a real danger in the corporate world, as business leaders may be blinded by hype or impressive case studies from technology suppliers. Instead of waddling along with the rest of the proverbial penguins, they should make their own, independent choices, not based on what their peers do or think, but rather based on their own research and data. For them to make such well-informed choices, CFOs must play a central role.

## Recognize that machines are better decision makers (7.3)

The robots are coming. And robots are also going to play an increasingly important role in decision-making. They will take over all standardized, regular decision-making as it can be programmed and is of a repetitive nature. This is a world apart for managers who normally make decisions based on experience, expertise, and intuition. They have to reinvent their relationship with these decision-making machines. And, above all, not be afraid to do so.

## 7.1  Look beyond the financial data

*Management information should be the indispensable fuel for making decision throughout the echelons of any organization. But reality is very different. Management information often consists of routinely drafted financial reports that nobody uses for decisions because they lack any real or valuable insights. This situation is unacceptable in an age where an unprecedented wealth of truly relevant information is readily available from within and outside of any organization.*

*It is also unacceptable in an age where leaders execute pur-pose-driven strategies rather than just focusing on maximizing financial performance, as society increasingly expects companies to be aware of their roles and responsibilities. More specifically, it is also unacceptable in times of crisis. When the proverbial shit hits the fan – ranging from financial distress to the sudden im-pact of a worldwide pandemic – organizations must look beyond traditional management information and think outside the box.*

*A radically different approach is therefore needed to generate management information and make decisions, one that really ensures managers will get a grip on how they can reach their strategic goals. An approach whereby management information is not based on traditional financial information, but rather on the entire ecosystem of data surrounding the organization. An approach that offers not only a good mirror on the past but mostly an excellent sensor for the future. Again, the question comes up: what can we learn from how Formula 1 teams have developed into Decision Oriented Organizations?*

'Twenty years ago, I joined a company that routinely produced a few thousand reports a month. Just stopped producing half of them. How many inquired about those stopped reports? Only a handful'.[74]

Signed, Ben Verwaaijen, former top executive at Alcatel-Lucent, British Telecom, and others.

With this tweet, he touched on a sore point. Many organizations have set up a real circus of reports; no one knows what purpose they serve let alone whether anyone really uses any of them. Nevertheless, many are too afraid to rigorously thin out the reporting jungle. During the research for this book, we spoke to a controller who told us that her department produced no fewer than 160 Key Performance Indicators (KPIs) for monthly reporting to the board. Within the organization, she had argued against producing such an excessive number as that would likely confuse rather than guide those for whom they were intended. But her proposal to substantially reduce the number did not make it – the board had been too afraid to make the change.

Obviously, producing 160 KPIs per month is probably a somewhat pointless exercise. And executives that are too afraid to stop such nonsense are really not worth their salt. The problem of inadequate management information is, however, a prevalent one and has a more deep-seated core than just its overkill of information. Their focus is also not in the right place, nor do they support decision-making as they are poor at showing which issues would be really relevant.

The rapid growth of WhatsApp is an example of this. The effect of the app on the revenue model of telecom companies only showed up in the management reports once it was too late. Another example in this sector would be the major upheaval that took place within 15 years in the market of telephone manufacturers. In 2000, Nokia, Motorola, Ericsson, Siemens, and Panasonic, in descending order, were the Big Five in this market. Within 15 years, the list changed completely to Samsung, Apple, Huawei, Oppo, and Xiaomi.

Business controllers should be interested to know when, during those 15 years, the boards of directors of the original Big Five first received any relevant management information about the threats on the horizon and were told about the often completely different market approach of those new competitors. In other words, who in this sector saw Xiaomi (founded in 2010) coming as a serious competitor, and when? The undercurrent of developments is often not visible in the multitude of EBITA figures, cash flow statements, and rolling revenue forecasts; even more concerning, these traditional tools often give a false sense of security. But it is precisely this undercurrent that would be the most relevant to the management and strategy of any organization.

## Small steps, giant leaps

Every organization should continuously monitor new behaviours, interests, and tools their consumers are starting to use. Even a small change in behaviour could signal a significant large, new overhaul in the industry. A seemingly small step may turn out to be a giant leap when it comes to winning or losing in a competitive market.

This is precisely why, at the start of the new season, Formula 1 teams are so eager to 'spy' on their competitors to see how they have developed during the winter break. In the spring of 2020, the defending world champion Mercedes team baffled analysts with a potentially revolutionary new steering system while testing in Barcelona. They noticed how Lewis Hamilton was pulling back the steering wheel of his Mercedes toward his body as he drove down the circuit's main straight and pushing the wheel back as he approached the first turn. What followed in the days after this test was a real frenzy of trying to decipher what Mercedes had developed.

## More data, better insights

'Impossible is nothing', boxing legend Muhamed Ali once said. This is also true when it comes to dishing out relevant information for decisions to managers and others. The increasing datafication of our world contributes to that. We can measure everything, from our heartbeat when jogging around the park, to the average processing time of a return shipment in a warehouse, to the real-time sentiment about a particular new product on social media. The abundance of data provides enormous insights that, in turn, can be used in decision-making processes in all sorts of areas and at all organizational levels. In theory, that is.

From here, we will give examples of the endless possibilities of data-driven decision-making and the technology that enables organizations to turn these possibilities into action. We will also analyse how changes in society affect corporate strategies and thereby the metrics for these strategies. After that we will share our thoughts on how to redesign management information to better suit the needs of an organization.

## Examples of using data for better decisions

A somewhat extreme example is that of a satellite used for analysing the state of the Russian grain fields; it takes photographs from space, twice a day. The images give an indication as to whether there are diseases or flooding events or forest fires that would affect the expected grain harvest. This information is then used by specialized agencies to predict market price developments, in combination with other kinds of data, of course. Such a satellite can also help in decision-making processes and forecasts in other areas. And then there is a company that monitors the occupancy rate at the immense parking lots of large US Walmart stores, also from space. Why would anyone do that? Because there is a link between the occupancy rate and Walmart's turnover, a link that can be valuable information for investors to use in their decision-making.

In other cases, less exotic technology is applied in data collection. For example, each month, stock market analysts eagerly await figures from payroll processor ADP. The volume of their salary processing turns out to be a good indicator of trends in unemployment. The indicator may not be quite as reliable as the official figures provided by government, but it is available much sooner and is therefore more relevant.

The previous examples concerned just external data sources. Many other cases, however, use internal data, which is then often combined with data from external sources. We see this in the case of supermarket chains that increasingly determine their product range on the basis of data, and adjust this range – fully automatically – on the basis of special circumstances. To put it simply, in the past, a supermarket manager relied on his or her experience to know how much extra beer and snacks to order in the run-up to any major national holiday, whereas today such decisions are determined by a system on the basis of a multitude of internal and external data. In addition, matters of assortment, shop layout, pricing, and promotions involve more and more mathematics.

In the logistics sector, too, converting a multitude of data sources into information that planners can base their decisions on may yield major benefits. UPS is one of the companies very committed to this approach, and its management believes that it is possible to cut down 160 million kilometres a year with data-driven decisions.[75]

The final example is one from an entirely different corner of the market; the insurance sector. Data on the insured population (their origins, profession, and many other characteristics) provide insight into present and future sickness benefit payments by health insurance and life insurance companies, and, thus, into profitability. The insight is vital because data is so much at the heart of business operations in these sectors. Every insurance product is, in fact, an algorithm that uses data to calculate the probability of certain events and their subsequent impact. The insurance company with the most accurate algorithm will be better at predicting their revenues and costs, and will take better decisions – which may put it ahead of the competition[76]. A real contemporary platform is Attune, a joint venture by AIG and Hamilton Insurance Group with hedge fund Two Sigma. This data and technology platform enables them to strongly refine pricing and selection of insurances in the SME segment of the market.

## Data-driven decisions means more than tooling

Data-driven decision-making is on the rise, with tools and techniques for fully or partially automating decision-making processes that are becoming increasingly more accurate, useful, and user-friendly. Just as we can get food from a vending machine whenever we feel like it, we can actually pull business insights out of a data lake when needed. The appealing thing here is that we can extract descriptive analyses as well as predictive modelling from the system. And it is precisely this predictive power of a data-driven approach that forms the basis for better decision-making.

As promising as that sounds, it is still a long way from reality. Many organizations are nowhere near ready to make actual data-driven decisions. In April of 2019, James Taylor, CEO of Decision Management Solutions, tweeted: 'Building good #analytics is not the hard part. Even deploying analytic models is not really hard anymore. EMPLOYING analytics to improve decision-making in the real world is the hard part'.[77]

This tweet underpins the core of what is needed to transform into a Decision Oriented Organization. Many organizations have already set up the necessary tools and platforms for many operational and tactical applications, but as soon as it comes to real management decisions that are a bit more strategic, the world looks very different. Business intelligence tooling has the potential to provide better insight for management in many organizations, but current practices for management information are far away from that potential.

**In times of crisis, the hunt for alternative data is on**
Our plea for a broader information spectrum proves to be especially true in times of turbulence. When everything is different, no business leader should be forced to take important decisions based on the usual information. Because as we all know: new problems can't be solved by old solutions.

This is why companies that excel in analysing a wealth of external and internal data are the best- performing ones in times of heavy turbulence. This became clear when the COVID-19 virus sent shock waves through society in early 2020. In hindsight, Dutch prime minister Mark Rutte chose wise words when he first addressed the nation about the Corona crisis. He was clear about the dilemmas that his government had to deal with: 'We have to make 100% of the decisions with 50% of the information.'

Many entrepreneurs and managers faced the same dilemmas in navigating their organizations through the uncharted territory caused by pandemic effects. Their world completely changed, and all traditional KPIs, from gross margins to customer satisfaction, were irrelevant to ensuring continuity in a crisis.

What they really wanted to know in the eye of the storm was, for example, what the cash flow for the coming weeks would look like and what financing scenarios were possible. Many information systems are poorly adapted to delivering such insights, although technology offers potential to unlock such information.

They also wanted to know about their customers' feelings or behaviours, how their competitors are doing, how logistics chains are affected, and where new or temporary opportunities are emerging in the market. Again: information systems often lack such insights, although technology offers potential to unlock such information

The mantra that one should never waste a good crisis applies when it comes to a new approach for management information. In the crisis, one needed to be creative to get relevant information on the table. That is crucial, because even in times of crisis one thing is certain: whoever makes the best decisions is the winner. And the best decisions require high-quality and relevant information. With a reference to Mark Rutte: if you have 51% of the information and your competitor has 50%, you could make the difference.

One of the promises of digital technology is that it can convert external data into such relevant information. An example from the beginning of the Corona crisis is that financial analysts used an intriguing series of data sources to gain insight into the economic consequences and thus their investment strategy. In their hunt for alternative data they used, among other things, GPS data from meal delivery companies and the development of smog levels to map economic activity in China.[78] Such 'sensors' to develop more grip in times of uncertainty are conceivable in many domains such as markets, products, consumer sentiment, payment data and many others. In fact, even the new reality of social distancing and thus collectively working from home led to a new application of such 'sensors'. According to *The Economist*[79], specialized tooling enabled insights in the completely new HR reality of large numbers of employees working from home. This varies from insights into changing workflows to measuring the sentiment and anxiety feelings among the employees who work from home. Such technology has been around for years: algorithms have for instance helped IBM with advice on pay rises and promotions and to pinpoint staff that is at risk of fleeing. In times of 'business unusual', such technology may become even more relevant.

### New metrics for a world in transition
Change is also underway from a different perspective: the model of management information and external accounting is in need of an overhaul to do justice to profound social changes. One of the signals that cannot be missed is that the

market value of a company has become disconnected from the figures in the financial accounts and/or quarterly reports; in fact, many value-driving factors cannot be found in the reports at all. Factories and capital have become a lot less decisive for that value, while 'softer' elements such as trust, a sustainable performance, social reputation, brands, and position in an ecosystem are gaining importance.

We should view this in relation to social changes. Harvard professor Michael Porter's 'conversion' actually sums it up well. For a long time, he was an avid supporter of shareholder value thinking, but around 2011 he adjusted his opinion quite drastically with his ideas about the new concept of Shared Value, which we mentioned earlier in Chapter 3: '(...) It will also reshape capitalism and its relationship to society. Perhaps most important of all, learning how to create shared value is our best chance to legitimize business again.'

According to him, the company of the future will be built on the concept of shared value, by contributing to economic profit and at the same time responding to the needs of the stakeholders. Since this conversion, the urgency of climate and other sustainability problems – which are essential in the concept of Shared Value – has also grown strongly worldwide. And with that, it is high time for a revolution in providing both internal and external information. More and more business leaders seek ways to focus explicitly on shared value (or in line with that: on the purpose of their organization). The current information provision based on financial information is not sufficient for this. The model needs to be converted to meet a much wider need for information.

Fortunately, this is no longer a hobby horse of sustainability experts; more and more mainstream investors want companies to provide them with information that gives a good picture of the long-term value creation. This gives a strong impulse for change. After all, investors can simply ignore companies that do not respond to their wishes and that puts these companies at a disadvantage in the capital market.

Clearly, real change calls for large parties to put their power behind the movement. And that is precisely why there seems to be a real shift. In 2018, CEO Larry Fink of investor Black-Rock made a remarkable call. He wants BlackRock – a serious player in the market with invested capital of US$6 trillion – to engage more in dialogue with the companies in which it invests. And at least as important, he wants companies to better explain what their strategy for long-term value creation looks like. Fink's remarks turned out not to be a one-off blip: at the beginning of 2020 he went a step further in his annual letter to chief executives at S&P 500 companies and large European corporations: BlackRock is getting stricter with companies that don't explain how they deal with climate change. The investment policy is also being made more sustainable, and investing in coal is partially banned.

The old saying that 'Money makes the world go around' thus gets a new meaning: the financial stimulus of the capital markets can force change towards sustainability in business, and thus also change the nature of reporting. This is one of the reasons for the interest in the concept of integrated reporting, in which financial reporting merges with reporting on other factors such as social factors. One of the major struggles with this is the lack of unambiguous standards on non-financial metrics. This may not be very surprising since it also took many decades before there was any uniformity in standards and definitions within financial reporting.

CFOs and the financial function in a broader sense therefore face the challenge of converting the information provision model. An important task. Because, as Peter Bakker, as chairman of the World Business Council for Sustainable Development, once said about the need for this new form of reporting, 'accountants can save the world'.

## Management information evolving beyond the financials

If we take the foregoing analysis of changing societal expectations and the evolution of data-driven techniques into account, there can be hardly any doubt: we must fundamentally alter the model of management information as it is the basis for decision-making. The core of management information, for now, still consists of financial data taken from the general ledger, the very type of information previously identified as *not* essential to good decision-making.

Think of this scenario: Formula 1 driver Max Verstappen would only have information on his current lap times during a race while not having information on the status of his tyres, the temperature of his brakes, potential weather changes, competing lap times, and other relevant data. He would in fact be clueless as to his chances of victory. Yet this is more or less a common situation in many organizations that build their management information largely on the general ledger. Formula 1 teams have found a way to combine hundreds of data points into information that guides them towards the best decisions on racing strategy. Most organizations are far away from being such a Decision Oriented Organization as they are still steering operations largely on financial information obtained from the general ledger.

It is a critical flaw in the design that appears very difficult to correct. A rather absurd situation, all things considered, since a general ledger is primarily a system that records transactions, not one that provides information. Important information comes from all sorts of places, both internal and external, in figures and not in figures, structured and unstructured. Making the best possible decisions means finding your way in this wealth of information.

> **The tap and the lake**
> Consultant Jyoti Banerjee has made a nice analogy between a water tap and a lake. 'Twentieth- century corporate reporting practice can be likened to a tap: the flows of information are periodic, uni-directional, and controllable by individual actors. In contrast, twenty-first century corporate information flows are more like a lake – all participants in the system have the opportunity to use the water (information) in the lake in multiple ways, including creating, distributing, and consuming corporate performance information'.[80]

Nevertheless, more than 20 years into the twenty-first century, the practice is still that financial departments have to deliver their peak performance once a month to present a monthly closing report and provide management information. They make every effort to deliver the most reliable information as quickly as possible. All this effort hopefully results in accurate data and management information. But, at the same time, that data is largely irrelevant for management to keep a grip on the future, which is why a reversal in the thinking about such information is needed.

What should be paramount in management information is not producing information but meeting informational needs. Although this sounds basic, the difference between these two is fundamental. It is even ingrained in the vocabulary of today's financial experts. They talk about reports as an outcome of their information production rather than as insights – input for the needs of the user.

### From Big Data to Big Information

Will this change? Almost certainly. The question is when. A new generation of managers is emerging who are better educated in data and analysis and who have very different expectations with regard to the information on which they base their decisions. They are not satisfied with standard reports but are looking for instant and tailor-made answers to any questions they may have. A finance function that excels in data collection and reporting no longer satisfies; instead, they want it to help them look ahead and provide them with insights through which they are able to take better decisions. They expect their finance function to guide them through the enormous amount of data and to separate the noise from the signal.

Moreover, pressure is mounting. In highly competitive markets, fuelled by the transparency of the Internet, a small difference may define who is winning and who is losing. Again, there is an interesting analogy with Formula 1 racing. The top league of the teams roughly have the same performance on the circuit, with differences in lap times sometimes being no more than a few fragments of a second. That's why having the best information as a basis for pit strategy or other decisions is so vital to end up as the winner. The same is true in many business sectors. And that's why transforming into a Decision Oriented Organization is a must.

As is almost always the case with such transformations, the rate of change is determined by the human factor, not by the state of technology. And things are not where they need to be with respect to the human element. Many studies into data-driven decision-making also conclude that the primary obstacle is neither the hardware nor the software; it is what some call wetware: Humans. According to a study from 2017, for example, 'Impediments include lack of organizational alignment, business and/or technology resistance, and lack of middle management adoption'.[81]

Many cultural changes are therefore needed before finance functions will truly be able to create a well-functioning decision-making system. Finance professionals themselves have to shake off their routines of collecting and recording financial data. To start with, they must increase their awareness of the types of insights needed in the decision-making processes that will determine the success of their company.

**Approximately right or exactly wrong**
One of the reasons that current management information is not really meeting management needs is that controllers have been educated and trained to ensure that information

should be correct and reliable. As a result, they will aim for 100% accuracy and invest large amounts of time and money in control frameworks and monthly financial administration. For the general ledger, this is also understandable and justified; it is a system in which invoices or stock mutations must be accurate. Put simply, an invoice needs to be correct, not 'roughly correct'.

For management information, however, this is not always necessary. Actually, a certain part of the information will never be exact. A famous quote from Alfred Einstein is inspiring in this respect: 'Not everything that counts can be counted. And not everything that can be counted counts'. John Maynard Keynes said something similar: 'I would rather be vaguely right than precisely wrong'.

These concepts are also very much to the point as far as management information is concerned. The sentiment about a new product on social media is probably not as easy to measure as sales figures, which are available down to the last decimal, but for decision-making, knowledge about the sentiment is probably much more important.

As the possibilities for using data – structured and unstructured – increase, the financial professionals must follow suit. The fact that reliability cannot always be guaranteed should not be an obstacle to this.

A fitting analogy is with one of Google's mantras: Quantity over Quality. The simple reasoning behind it is that all errors in data can be solved by adding more data. Google is not aiming to increase the quality of the original data (and it is in no position to do so, anyway), but instead it aims for larger amounts of data that can be combined with the right algorithms and can thus be tested for reliability.

In doing so, they need to cast off the yoke of accuracy (see the text box). The most important thing here is the overall picture, which is created by combining large amounts of data from a multitude of internal and external sources. Sources that cannot always be checked for reliability.

## Stop using the general ledger

There's no doubt that changing the information management model begins with changing the mindset of the professionals who are responsible for it. CFOs wanting to build a Decision Oriented Organization must seriously investigate the possibilities for a radically different approach to management information. A nice exercise would perhaps be to ask their finance staff members to complete the seemingly simple task of drafting a financial report without using a general ledger.

That may sound like a crazy idea, but the greatest successes often come from thinking 'outside the box'. For example, who would have thought that a restaurant that does not supply its diners with any cutlery could go on to become one of the world's largest restaurant chains (McDonald's)? Or, would you have believed beforehand that a random, global collection of volunteers could build a reliable encyclopaedia (Wikipedia)? And who would have thought that a mobile telephone could do without a keyboard and that this would become the standard (Apple)?

We need more imagination when it comes to management information, too. The financial world could do with a Steve Jobs.

## Core messages to CFOs:

✓ **Do not consider what information is available; consider what information is needed**

A management report is not a summary of financial systems, but should meet the informational needs of management so that they can make the right decisions. If you could walk a mile in the shoes of a manager, you would likely develop a completely different management report, providing completely different types of information. Executives are mainly interested in knowing how markets, innovations, and customer expectations are developing.

✓ **Dare to thin out the reporting forest**

Adding KPIs is simple and leads to an impressive volume and diversity of management reports. But it turns out that more courage is needed to thin out this forest.

✓ **Choose 'approximately right', rather than exactly wrong**

Reliability and accuracy down to the last decimal is important in invoicing but not for generating management information, at least not always.

✓ **Change the mindset**

The pace of change is often determined by the human factor rather than by technological advances. Finance professionals must grasp the new reality of management information.

## 7.2 Don't be a penguin

*Humans are herd animals. Probably much more than you think. Humans are extremely sensitive to what other people do and what they think about our ideas. This is also true when it comes to choices about new information technology. Many companies get carried away by technology hype and impressive stories told by technology vendors, with many disappointments and failed projects as a result.*

*This is one of the elements involved in decision-making that really needs to change as well. Executives should not be penguins waddling along with the rest of the penguins, but rather, and above all, learn to think critically and make independent choices that are based on their own opinions and research. Because only then, will new technology indeed contribute to better information, better decisions, and, in turn, the ability to distinguish. CFOs play a pivotal role in securing these well-informed choices about new technology, as they are the common-sense thinkers and analytical conscience of the organization.*

When Bill Gates was still at the helm of Microsoft, he retreated for a week each year and literally locked himself away in a log cabin on the American West Coast with a pile of ideas, white papers, and articles that employees had sent him. Documents that would advocate internal changes, innovations, or strategic choices. During these so-called Think Weeks, Gates used to go through all the material, adding his comments to the documents and sometimes making crucial strategic decisions based on the analyses. A famous example is the Tidal Wave memo he wrote in 1995. The memo left no room for misinterpretation: the Internet was going to shake the industry to its core.

David A. Kaplan's book *The Greatest Business Decisions of All Time* recounts how Gates did exactly this, and how he gradually put in place an infrastructure to allow communications to flow back to the entire organization. An important side effect of his annual Think Week was the example this was setting; Gates showed the entire organization how important he thought it was to generate and assess ideas on the basis of independent thinking, without any yes-men around him. In an article in the *Wall Street Journal*, the Think Week was called 'the world's coolest suggestion box' for good reason. In his book, Kaplan wrote this on the subject: 'Though ideas were key for Gates, he well understood the morale effect that Think Week could have on employees'.

**Unfollow the hype**
It is rather strange, come to think of it, that the Think Week concept did not catch on more than it did, especially in a world where one technology hype follows the next, and where trend watchers, consultants, and authors of management books take to the stage to broadcast the latest buzzwords. From machine learning to blockchain, from Internet of Things to Augmented Reality, from scrums to data lakes to Robotic Process Automation; every single one of those is important, of course, and all have great potential, but in the tsunami of new technological concepts, it is quite complicated to separate the wheat from the chaff and not blindly follow every hype.

This is precisely why it is so important for leaders to analyse new technology themselves, just as Gates did (and reportedly still does in his post-CEO period). However, many organizations and their executives are downright terrible at this. Many become blinded by the shiny objects offered them in the way of new information technology. Below we discuss three factors that play a role here: people's fear of leaving the herd, flawed group dynamics, and inadequate data collection used in making crucial decisions.

### Fear of leaving the herd

As mentioned earlier, people are herd animals. When out walking with others, our limbs will automatically synchronize without anyone even noticing. Often, when we yawn, lean forward, or cough during a conversation, so too will our conversation partners, usually unconsciously. And when one person runs away in a panic, we all start running in the same direction without first giving it much thought. Even those who think they are insensitive to herd behaviour. A beautiful scene from the Monty Python classic, *Life of Brian* (1979), makes this herd behaviour painfully clear. In the movie, the main character is followed by a crowd that thinks he is the new messiah. Speaking from a balcony, he tries to talk sense to them, urging them to think for themselves. 'You're all individuals!', he tells them, upon which the crowd roars back: 'We're all individuals!'.

Such herd-like behaviour plays an important role in business as well. Many organizations do more or less the same thing. In a figurative sense, they are all penguins. Cute animals, but they all look alike. They waddle in rows, one after the other, all choosing the same rockface to hatch their eggs and often diving into the water at the same time. Completely routinely, without thinking.

Among managers, such herd-like behaviour is largely born out of fear or uncertainty. This is not very surprising. When consultants and colleagues all tell you about how Robotic Process Automation is an amazing way to save costs in your financial department, as CFO you will soon come to believe it. After all, you would be crazy to pass up such an opportunity to save money, and people may think you are a fool for not doing so. The same goes for novelties in other departments, such as marketing and human resources.

Without many managers wanting to admit to it openly, they often apply the cover-your-arse principle. Choosing the safe option, and making sure no one will be able to blame them if things go wrong. Leaving the herd by going with the less obvious option means all eyes will be on them and mistakes can be career-ending. Managers brave enough to deviate from standard practice, thus, are putting their corporate lives at risk.

There is a fitting reference to the history of software. Around 1998, open-source operating system Linux started to weaken the position of traditional software on the market. The term *open-source* was still exotic at the time, and Linux was mainly seen as something pimply faced teenagers were using when they were fooling around with a soldering iron on their PCs motherboard. The question of whether open-source products one day could compete with the products of Blue Chip companies, therefore, was being met with sarcasm from the corporate world. CIOs who were opting for the unknown open-source products were quite literally risking their careers.

Two decades later, more or less the reverse is true. Open-source is no longer the domain of spotty adolescents but has penetrated professional environments. In fact, data scientists are considering open-source to be the norm. And IBM is spending US$34 billion to acquire Red Hat, one of the early pioneers of open-source. These days, anyone not opting for open-source solutions has some explaining to do, as the open-source philosophy – open collaboration without central ownership – has proven to lead to high quality. In 2019, the salient title of an article on ZDNet, which discussed the takeover of Red Hat by IBM, says it all: 'Can Red Hat save IBM?'[82]

## Flawed group dynamics

The best decisions are often made by a collaboration of minds rather than by a single individual. But this only works if the group of minds contains a sufficient variety of personality traits. In many organizations, it is precisely this mix that is absent from the boardroom. An overrepresentation of psychopaths may also be at the root of the problem. Viewed across the population as a whole, approximately 1 in 100 people could be diagnosed a psychopath. Perhaps surprisingly, among top executives (and detainees [sic]), this share is estimated to be 4 in 100.[83]

This particular type of executive is highly driven and allows nothing and no one to stop them from achieving their goal. Professor Manfred Kets de Vries calls them SOBs in a research paper, which in his case stands for Seductive Operational Bully. The professor is unsparingly critical in his characterization of this group: 'These SOB Executives can be inspiring, charming, seductive, but also extremely Machiavellian. They are prepared to trample the bodies of their weaker colleagues, taking credit for the work they have done and scapegoating them when things go wrong. There's nothing they won't do and no one they won't exploit to get what they want. They will manipulate financial results, plant rumours, turn co-workers against each other, and alter their persona as needed to destroy their targets. They can be irresistible, with an uncanny ability to seduce others into seeing and doing things their way'.[84]

These character traits cause such psychopaths to also be responsible for numerous corporate scandals. For this book, however, the last sentence of his quote is particularly relevant: psychopaths (and narcissists, also over-represented in these circles) limit the freedom of thought and judgement that would lead to making good team decisions – including about investments in information technology.

In such cases, there is often insufficient knowledge available to take good decisions. That deficiency can be solved if there is a willingness to investigate, look at all the facts, learn, and listen to others. Which is exactly what Bill Gates did during his Think Weeks. However, in boardrooms controlled by psychopaths, this very skill is rather hard to come by.

### 600% better decisions?

One of the shortcomings in decision-making is that many considerations are often binary; there are only two options: 'Should I do A, yes or no?' Research shows that considerations with more than two choices ('Should I choose A, B, or C?') lead to much better decisions. Paul Nutt (Ohio State University) at the end of the last century showed that only a minority of teams are looking for decision-making on the basis of multiple alternatives, which actually frustrates decision-making.[85] In the long term, 'go'-'no go' decisions do not work out well. For decisions based on multiple alternatives, the failure rate was 32%. This makes sense. After all, if a manager pursues a particular option, everything will be aimed at making that idea succeed, rather than being used to study whether there would also be an even better option. This is a lesson that is also important in investments in new technology or systems and, in some cases, will prove to be a rather practical way of making better decisions. Adding more options leads to better decisions – up to 600% better, in fact, according to Patrick McDaniel, US expert on decision-making.[86]

## Inadequate data collection

Good information fuels good decisions. But things can also go wrong, particularly when gathering information. One of the problems is that we draw conclusions based on information that is right in front of us such as glossy reports by technology producers and consultants. Other information, outside our immediate field of vision, is not or is insufficiently taken into account. This problem is at the root of the failure of numerous large technology projects. Business cases are formulated, but they are often not really based on the most relevant information.

Famous psychologists confirm this human inbred behaviour. Daniel Kahneman, author of *Thinking, Fast and Slow* and founder of behavioural economics, speaks about narrow framing and calls this a major problem for good decision-making. In his book, *Enlightenment Now*, Steven Pinker writes about how it does not take much for human beings to arrive at a very distorted view of reality. His analysis: whoever follows the news closely cannot have a good picture of the state of the world. After all, news is about incidents rather than trends. A breached dyke is news, slowly rising sea levels is not, or only marginally. The media is filled with stories about fraud, but it tells us very little about slowly professionalizing financial management. Whoever is keeping up with the news should not confuse this with obtaining a good picture of reality.

## Hype & Hope around blockchain

Blockchain aptly illustrates how managers can get carried away and make decisions irrationally. Blockchain began to attract massive interest around 2015. However, more often than not, hype and hope appeared to outweigh realism. A typical example from 2017 is that of the US biotechnology company Bioptix which changed its name to Riot Blockchain and promptly saw its share price skyrocket. Another sign of the times is the almost infinite number of blockchain believers preaching the gospel from equally as many pulpits. If their stories are to be believed, blockchain may be the solution to almost any problem. Idealists, for example, see the possibilities of blockchain reuniting underage refugees with their parents or putting an end to atrocious working conditions in Congolese mines. The optimism is reminiscent of the dotcom hype that took hold of the world at the end of last century. Hordes of people were convinced that we were entering a completely new world in which economic recessions were a thing of the past. They were wrong.

Could the same be happening around blockchain – could it put an end to the big dreams about the related decentralization? The fact is that many entrepreneurs see blockchain as an opportunity, whether or not goaded into it by trend watchers. Banks are in fierce competition, fearful of missing the boat. But blockchain also and emphatically plays a role outside the financial sector. For example, in a pilot project where blockchain is applied in maternity care; in an app based on blockchain, parents can approve the number of hours worked by the maternity nurse. An article on the Dutch health care website *Zorgvisie*, reports that this pilot has raised questions, and there is some uncertainty about blockchain being the dreamed-of solution: 'Improvements in maternity care could be achieved, in part, by using techniques other than blockchain', according to those involved.[87]

They are hitting the nail on the head. Blockchain technology is often a cumbersome solution to a problem that could just as well (or better!) be solved in other ways, i.e. using conventional information technology and databases. Decentralization sounds nice but is often also very inefficient. In fact, blockchain solutions are sometimes even sought for solving non-existing problems.

This can also be translated to the realm of executives and all the technology hype that lands on their desks. Studying each of those does provide a picture of all the new things on offer, but hardly shows what happens behind the scenes, nor does it reveal the general impact of digital technology on the playing field. While this would actually be interesting knowledge to have.

## Soapbox

On this subject, Pinker believes that the only way to really know what is going on in the world is by counting things yourself. How many people are sick, illiterate, undernourished, or poor? This is also what executives should be doing – separate the wheat from the chaff with regard to technology. They need to analyse those new technological innovations for themselves, and not become enchanted by a random expert on a soapbox. Because such isolated success stories are a very limited source of information, and certainly offer no guarantees about the success of the next application.

Moreover, who is to say that a success story is representative of a particular new technology? Maybe that one success story was preceded by 100 failed attempts, and its success was the result of other factors than the use of that particular technology? These questions, however, are rarely asked during the social events that follow such dazzling presentations. And so, the information value of successful cases is greatly overestimated and could really only be meaningful if its failures were also known and could be analysed. Every self-respecting scientist knows that entire populations need to be analysed before meaningful conclusions about anything can be drawn. It is the only way to obtain a realistic picture. In the domain of management and technology hype, however, this law of nature is consistently being sinned against.

## Most CFOs are other CFOs

*Most people are other people*, as Oscar Wilde once said. People have a tendency to imitate each other's behaviour and parrot each other's opinions. Analogous to Wilde's quote, we could also say, 'Most CFOs are other CFOs'. And that is a serious problem in today's world with its far-reaching transformations, where CFOs need to make their own choices.

The three factors outlined earlier – the fear of leaving the herd, flawed group dynamics, and Inadequate data collection – play an important role in this respect.

CFOs play a key role in improving this situation and can do so from their inherent critical attitude. Improvements start with acknowledging the underlying human inbred behaviour.

## Core messages to CFOs:

✓ **Provide an environment that stimulates outside-the-box behaviour**
'If you want to change the game, stop following the rules.' Nothing is as killing as an environment in which no one dares to deviate from the norm. It creates the giant risk that decisions are mostly dominated by fear of failure rather than by opportunities.

✓ **Organize resistance**
No shine without friction. Critical and debunking questions are needed to get to the heart of any matter. A diverse team – including multiple disciplines – may help to ensure that decisions are studied from all angles.

✓ **Look beyond the obvious**
The human brain tends to jump to conclusions, because we use information that is right in front of us but are rather blind to anything else that requires a little more effort.88 CFOs and their teams are able to contribute from their professionally critical roles, actively look for arguments *against* a certain decision, and question it in order to have the right discussion.

## 7.3  Recognize that machines are much better decision-makers

*As discussed in the previous chapter, human inbred behaviour puts great pressure on good decision-making. This has always been the case, but in a world full of data, where decisions are becoming much more explicit, an additional issue is also involved. Managers were used to making decisions from a mix of experience, expertise and intuition. In the new situation, they would have to give up their autonomy to a machine that makes decisions based on data and pre-programmed decision rules. The question is: are they ready to do this? And, if so, how do we keep people in the decision-making loop?*

A man and a woman are seated at a table, having dinner, glass of wine in hand. The man says dryly, 'Let me interrupt your expertise with my confidence.' This is a cartoon in the *New Yorker* about mansplaining which went viral in 2018. With the rise of Artificial Intelligence, the woman in the cartoon could be replaced by a machine. Because even though the hard data-based decisions made by machines are demonstrably better than those made by humans, it is still difficult for many managers to actually hand those decisions over to the machine.

They are still very much convinced that they are right.

The relationship between human and machine is a hot item in these times of rapid technological development. An impressive list of scientists and entrepreneurs – e.g. Bill Gates, the late Stephen Hawking, Elon Musk – have been warning for years of the dangers of AI and how it poses a great risk to humankind. For film writers and directors in Hollywood, this is a rewarding subject for dystopian scenarios. In contrast, there are many other experts who do not believe things will go all that fast and that, probably more importantly, humans will be able to tame the technology and control it while it reaches maturity.

Unfortunately, there is no crystal ball to tell us how this scenario will unfold, but one thing is certain; the discussion has an impact on the theme of this book: how we make decisions.

Many managers and directors are reluctant to entrust important decisions to technology, which is one of the reasons why the real benefits of digital technology have not yet been reaped.

Looking only at the facts, we can see an unequal battle unfolding between human and machine, in this context.

The human brain is able to handle only a limited amount of data and complexity. In fact, research[89] shows that most of our decisions are not even made consciously, but are handled by subconscious mental activity. The subconscious has a greater processing capacity. The notion of 'sleeping on it' before taking a difficult decision is, therefore, often not only a good idea but also a scientifically substantiated good idea.[90]

Machines do not go to sleep at night, nor do they have to. With their great computing power, they are able to make decisions based on an infinite number of variables, and by applying machine learning techniques, they can improve those decisions over the course of time.

Simply put, machines can make better decisions than humans.

It is precisely this conclusion that Daniel Kahneman draws in his book *Thinking Fast and Slow*. He concludes that in uncertain and unpredictable situations, humans lose to machines. In an impressive number of areas 'the longevity of cancer patients, the length of hospital stays, the diagnosis of cardiac disease, and the susceptibility of babies to sudden infant death syndrome; economic measures such as the prospects of success for new businesses, the evaluation of credit risks by banks, and the future career satisfaction of workers; questions of interest to government agencies, including assessments of the suitability of foster parents, the odds of recidivism among juvenile offenders, and the likelihood of other forms of violent behaviour; and miscellaneous outcomes such as the evaluation of scientific presentations, the winners of football games, and the future prices of Bordeaux wine'.[91]

This also makes it clear that human intuition and experience do not contribute to better decisions. We have to convince managers not to rely on their own judgement and to acknowledge that machines can do better. 'Unfollow your stomach', as Viktor Mayer Schonberger, author of several bestsellers on data, put it during an interview in the summer of 2019.[92] This may feel a bit unsettling for many, and at this point we may once more get back to the Formula 1 analogy. Remember how Sebastian Vettel was bemoaning the fact that computers were better at predicting the fastest lines on a circuit? He is not too happy with that, but in the Formula 1 world there is simply no alternative. He must 'unfollow his stomach' and acknowledge the decision power of the computational models.

However, all of this by no means signifies that people will be sidelined in the decision-making process. Humans and digital machines do need to find a new way of using data, together, to arrive at the best decisions. Traditionally, people take the results from data-driven models into account in their decision-making processes and the machine provides them with input. But it would be far more effective to do this exactly the other way around; in other words people provide input for the machines and this will lead to those machines making increasingly better decisions. As Chapter 6 described, knowledge of the context is essential when basing decisions on data analysis and this is what people can bring to the table.

**Flying in the clouds**
Aviation offers an inspiring analogy for the relation between humans and machines. Basically, there are two types of flight regulations for navigation. A pilot can fly on sight, according to the so-called Visual Flight Rules (VFR). This is possible if there is sufficient visibility to determine position. A fully trained and certified pilot can also fly according to the Instrument Flight Rules (IFR). He or she will then be guided by the instruments.

Human expertise remains of great importance in training computer models and in asking the right questions, and people are better at it, at least for now. Moreover, they also have a much stronger associative ability when compared to digital machines. If people are presented with various layers of information (numbers, images, text, and other types of information), they will ask questions about the information and are able to see logical patterns that a machine cannot see.

Such new collaborations between humans and digital machines are a major ingredient for building a Decision Oriented Organization. One could wonder how relevant the issue is, seeing that the advancement of digital technology such as AI is certainly not yet mainstream. 'They promised us flying cars and instead we got 140 characters', Peter Thiel once joked about the technological revolution. If we are honest about the revolution of digital innovations such as AI, we see something similar going on. Artificial intelligence could totally disrupt every imaginable human activity, but frankly speaking, this revolution has so far been a pretty tame affair.

This can probably not be regarded separate from the previous argument: people find it difficult to see machines as fully fledged partners when it comes to making decisions. If we focus exclusively on developing the technology and fail to pay attention to changing the way people make decisions, the AI revolution will remain rather minor. It is time to place managers next to machines.

## Core messages to CFOs:

✓ **Convince managers that their instincts often do not yield the best decisions**

The job of managers is changing. When they make decisions, managers are accustomed to relying strongly on their intuition and experience. Artificial intelligence will only be able to deliver on its promises if managers are willing to change their professional behaviour and allow AI to play a role.

✓ **Position the manager next to the machine instead of on the opposite side**

Machines are better than people at using data to unravel complex decisions. But because, at least for the time being, people are better than machines at identifying relationships and questioning situations, the best decisions are made when people and machines work together.

# Chapter 8  Organizing

FROM
a rigid and compartmentalized structure
TO
an adaptive and connected network

*In a dynamic environment, many decisions cannot be put off until tomorrow. This calls for flexible organizational structures. Traditional hierarchical pyramids – in which an aggregate of information first flows upwards before decisions are made – are too slow. In addition, many organizations are still highly compartmentalized, without smooth collaboration between their individual departments.*

*Yet another comparison with Formula 1 racing demonstrates clearly the main challenge of change. During a race, Formula 1 teams are processing information about conditions as they change, ranging from impending showers to a sudden pit stop by a competitor or a crash resulting in a safety car situation – information that they subsequently and directly convert into decisions about their car and whatever needs to happen in the continuation of the race. In other words, decisions about the immediate future. The teams, with their direct and horizontal type of organization, work with predefined scenarios and related decision rules, which means that vital decisions can be made on the spot and data is shared in a seamless process between experts within and outside these teams.*

*The central question in this chapter, therefore, reads: how could CFOs build decision-oriented organizations that are as flexible as those Formula 1 teams and do not suffer from any compartmentalization?*

Over the past decade, a small but impactful revolution has been taking place in software development. We are talking DevOps[93] here; a name that combines software development (Dev) and information technology operations (Ops). It includes a fairly rigorous change in software development. Traditionally, following the so-called waterfall method, this involves long-term processes (functional design, programming, and testing) in departments specifically created for this purpose, with new software not being implemented until the testing phase has been successfully completed. With DevOps, the process is very different. It may actually be very insightful to learn from DevOps more broadly while building a Decision Oriented Organization.

First, let's examine the concept a bit more. In a nutshell, it comes down to software being developed not within a separate test environment but with modifications immediately going live. If a modification works satisfactorily, the new version will remain in place; if not, the modification is withdrawn. The essential element is the direct feedback on results, boosting flexibility and speed to a considerable degree. The process is not only a 'technical adjustment' of working methods, but also, and above all, a 'cultural shift'.

The power of such concepts has been proven at Google. Part of their success lies in the philosophy for many of its products – known as 'Always in Beta'. At companies such as Amazon,

Booking.com, and Uber, this comes to the fore in so-called A/B testing; systems are adjusted daily for continuous optimization. Website users – the customers – are the actual testers. This is a world away from the waterfall approach in which months are often spent working on new pieces of software which are then extensively tested before going live. This fast way of working offers much more flexibility and is reserved not only for start-ups, but can be seen in all shapes and forms throughout the business community. It is successful only if all those involved collaborate closely and if there are no 'walls' between the various disciplines.

**Contrast**
This relatively new approach to software development may serve as an inspiring example for setting up decision-making processes to also be fast and flexible. First of all, because the example shows how decisions and adjustments can be turned into a continuous process, with autonomy at low levels in the organization. And in second place, because DevOps requires closer collaboration between specialists; a compartmentalized approach is simply impossible with DevOps because the model only works if there is a seamless dialogue and feedback between those specialists.

These are exactly the two things that are needed, in a generic sense, to make decisions that are more data driven. Because organizations that have a perfect set up for data analysis but are unable to deal with it are wasting their money on such infrastructure.

This chapter discusses the related two topics:

**Reset management control: PDCA every day** (8.1) Here, the traditional steps of the plan-do-check-act cycle merge and accelerate. Instead of being a monthly exercise, it is a permanent process that constantly forces you to look ahead. It calls for an entirely different approach to management control in which information is translated directly into action. It also calls for a very different set-up of the finance function, with fewer controllers and more data scientists.

**Connect the data dots** (8.2) Data analysis offers endless possibilities, but what looks perfect on the drawing board does not always come true in practice, partly because work is still being done too much in isolated silos. Decompartmentalization is needed; the use of data needs to be considered 'end to end'. And such 'end-to-end' thinking does not stop at the boundaries of an organization or department, but needs to be based on an organization's entire ecosystem. All this starts with a decompartmentalized organization that resembles a network rather than a traditional hierarchical structure.

## 8.1 Reset management control: PDCA every day

*Business economics in the twenty-first century is an extremely unpredictable reality. In that reality, hardly anything can be taken for granted and surprises are a daily occurrence. Competitors emerge from other sectors, new technology completely changes business models from one day to the next, and markets can be totally unpredictable – due to a tweet from a world leader, for example. The cycle of planning & control, however, is often still based on the old, predictable reality. This is why it is high time for a thorough reset of the PDCA cycle.*

Many financial experts will associate the name William Deming with the management cycle that bears his name. The Deming plan-do-check-act (PDCA) cycle was developed in the middle of the previous century and still plays an important role today in systematic management and improvement of organizations. It is a methodical way of strategic planning. Monthly management information plays a central role, as this information is vital in making adjustments. In practice, though, there are drawbacks to this as the nature of the information often doesn't serve the objectives well (see also Chapter 5).

The PDCA cycle was developed to manage and adjust activities in a fairly stable and predictable environment. In many sectors, however, such stability and predictability are hard to come by, and it is therefore rather amazing that the cycle has hardly been adapted to modern standards.

*Exactly how do these modern standards differ from those of the past?*
First of all, the continual wave of new technology in combination with digitization has major consequences. Technological developments no longer just increase process efficiency – the removal of friction is actually the basis of many of Silicon Valley's great successes – but also lead to a flow of new products, services, and business models that completely change the market and until recently were unthinkable. For example, consider the way in which platform companies have completely changed the market of traditional players, a development that we analysed in Chapter 2. Business models of existing parties are in fact continuously 'hacked' by challengers.

The second difference is based on the other reasons for markets to change completely within a short period of time. Markets can also be influenced by things like a tweet from a world leader or a sudden social outcry about an incident that is spreading unchecked. This is exacerbated by societal impatience and lack of trust. Reputations can therefore be lost rather quickly.

Thirdly, the traditional relative safety of a large organization has been greatly reduced. Particularly in a digital world, good ideas by small start-ups can have an enormous impact on established large market players in a short period of time. For this reason, those established players cannot afford to rest on their laurels, not even for a moment.

The fourth and final difference is that not only the business environment but also the character of organizations themselves is undergoing dramatic change. This can be seen in how companies are increasingly collaborating with other parties within ecosystems, often in rapidly changing coalitions. It is visible in how IT developments are dominating virtually all areas of business – software is 'eating the world'.[94] And it can also be seen in how a new generation of employees enjoys experimentation and thinks far less in blueprints. This combination of internal changes also makes the conventional planning & control cycle feel like a tight squeeze.

### Moving from plantation to rainforest

In summary, the old business-as-usual situation can be considered as a well-organized 'plantation', where yields are optimized in a structured way and known diseases are being fought. The new 'business unusual' situation is, roughly translated from the book by Victor Hwang and Greg Horowitt, more like a chaotic rainforest[95] where no day is like another and enemies and diseases loom each and every day. Those trying to survive in this rainforest using the 'tooling' of the plantation will be sorely disappointed since the old tooling was devised with efficient conveyor belt production in mind or to optimize the sales apparatus. It was not designed to forge an immediate answer to a start-up that thinks it can completely disrupt your market with a new proposition or respond to a tweet from a president who makes the markets tremble.

And yet, this is exactly what many companies continue to do in their management control cycle. In the white paper that formed the basis for their book,[96] Hwang and Horowitt write: 'A company that seeks to manufacture cheaper, better, more profitable laptop computers would run operations like an agricultural plantation. It would seek to control and tune all of the specific processes for producing that computer to the finest degree possible. However, a community that seeks to generate high levels of innovation throughout the whole system would do the opposite. It would run operations like a rainforest, not controlling the specific processes but instead helping to set the right environmental variables that foster the unpredictable creation of new weeds.'

## A much-needed reset of management control
The same applies to the management control cycle. What would the desired reset look like? First of all, the cycle needs to be radically accelerated. It goes without saying that in this rainforest, management cannot use monthly meetings to ensure their company survives based on some indicator results; survival depends on permanent and continued management

control – i.e. PDCA every day. It is about making adjustments on the basis of a continuous feedback loop.

Secondly, the management control cycle needs to focus far more on the future than it does today. Many current management reports of course also contain forecast information, but as most CFOs would confirm, the focus is mainly on comparing budget against actuals. Although that is also an important analysis, it is one that is not very relevant for successful survival in the said rainforest.

The third factor flows from the second: more attention needs to be paid to 'soft' information. Management control currently focuses on 'hard' facts. This is in itself a commendable aim – because discussions are best conducted on the basis of facts – but it does not do justice to the essence of management control. After all, essential information about future factors is not always factual, first, because this information is often a little softer, but also, and perhaps even more importantly, because good management control also requires a keen insight into the underlying drivers of factual information. It is much more relevant to know roughly *why* the turnover is growing than to know exactly by *how much* it is growing.

This leads to the important question of how CFOs could ensure that this management control cycle is revamped. What needs to be done to make sure the cycle lives up to the standards required for a Decision Oriented Organization? Again, this hinges on three factors.

*1. Management control needs to shift from the hierarchical top to the entire organization*

A wide variety of organizations are reinventing themselves with concepts such as self-governance, holacracy,[97] networking, and all types of agile concepts. 'Unbossing' is what all these concepts have in common. A world is emerging in which the pyramids (i.e. the hierarchical organizations) are losing out to the new 'flatbreads' (i.e. the organic networks without hierarchical leadership). This new world nevertheless also needs certain instruments to keep abreast of what is happening and be able to act whenever necessary. Perhaps even more than ever, good management control is what is required. Management control therefore needs to be shifted from the hierarchical top to the entire organization.

In this context, many managers need to master the art of letting go. An analogy with self-driving cars illustrates this point; the vehicles are fitted with numerous sensors to enable them to react immediately in unexpected situations, for example, if a toddler suddenly crosses the road or a lorry loses its load onto the road surface. And they are better at it than human drivers. We should design the management control of organizations in the same way. The required technology to use such 'sensors' for management control is already available; we need to see if management is ready to hand over the steering wheel. Our conversations with C-suite members[98] sometimes revealed an astonishing reality. Leaders who do not hesitate to make factories or logistic operations more efficient or intelligent appear to be terrified about implementing a similar 'smartification' of management tasks such as financial control.

In reality, all phases in the traditional PDCA cycle could be handled by new technology such as Machine Learning and Artificial Intelligence. The pace at which this would happen is not determined by what the technology can do, but rather depends on the personal courage and determination of the C-suite members.

## 2. Inverting the pyramid in the finance function

The second requirement is a total revamp of the financial function. Originally, this function was at the heart of the management control cycle because this cycle originally had a strong financial focus and only later included a wealth of other types of information.

The new reality of data and digital technology should really include do-it-yourself options for the users of information everywhere within the organization. This is a world away from the current situation in many organizations, where business units often still have their own controllers who are responsible for data collection, processing, and interpretation. These positions will largely become extinct in the future. The finance function will be centralized and will only facilitate do-it-yourself (DIY) management control. The character of the work in financial departments is expected to change dramatically, as shown in figure 8.1.

**Vision of Finance Transformation**
From daily routine to supporting growth and new business models

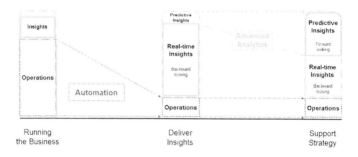

Figure 8.1 Vision of finance transformation

This also means the need for a finance function with completely different types of knowledge and competencies. The work of administrators and controllers is becoming more and more automated and is a hygiene factor. A new breed of professionals will capture data of all kinds, using various types of sensors. At the same time, the need is growing for data specialists who are able to build predictive models that all users can work with themselves. It is also not inconceivable that the finance function of the future will be referred to in terms of 'performance support', 'value challenger', or 'business navigator' – terms that are already starting to emerge today.

*3. Focus on* learning *instead of* checking *in the PDCA cycle*
The third factor is the PDCA cycle itself. According to some, the model is no longer fit for purpose because it is considered rigid. Its original purpose was to manage and adjust activities in order to achieve as many of the strategic goals as possible. In today's world, change is a continual process and planning and controlling is in fact impossible, if only because strategic

goals are also moving targets. In other words, the PDCA cycle suffices for the plantation, but not for the rainforest.

The problem with how the PDCA cycle is currently applied is not only its slow pace, but also that, over time, the concept has acquired a typical 'in control' approach. The bookkeeping approach of being 'in control' has a strong internal focus, which is mainly about ensuring that an organization is able to control the internal flows of money and goods. However, the relevance of this approach is only limited, both to management and capital investors. Traditional 'in-control thinking' is actually only sufficient in a business-as-usual environment. For a company that operates in a fairly stable environment (i.e. the plantation), control is important to prevent unexpected financial events and to properly set up controlling aspects so that the information system is in order (and remains so). But as soon as there is business unusual – e.g. a crisis, rapidly changing market conditions, or a drastic reorganization – the concept is much less relevant.

In the rainforest, therefore, organizations need to be in control of rapid external changes. This calls for good feedback mechanisms to translate developments into corrective measures. The PDCA cycle could provide that feedback mechanism if the C of 'check' is interpreted to mean the ability to *learn* rather than to *check*.

And the final and probably most remarkable detail: a bit of historic research shows that the Deming PDCA cycle does not even exist…What is this all about? Deming developed the PDSA cycle with the S for 'study'. It was a Japanese engineer who, years later, converted Deming's concept into something we all now – erroneously – call the Deming PDCA cycle. Deming was himself very clear about the connection between the PD-SA and PDCA cycles: 'They bear no relation'. In 1990, 40 years after he first conceived his model, he wrote, 'be sure to call it PDSA, not the corruption PDCA'.[99] Now, another 30 years later, perhaps it is time that we start doing so. Because the original model – which focuses on 'study' rather than 'checking' – actually fits in much better with today's needs.

## Core messages to CFOs:

✓ **Start viewing the external environment as a rainforest rather than a plantation**

In the past, the external environment was a well-organized 'plantation', figuratively speaking, where structured yields were optimized. Today's environment is more comparable to a rainforest where enemies and diseases loom every day. Survival calls for different management controls with tooling that is faster and more forward looking.

✓ **Don't position management control as a job for the hierarchical top**

'Unbossing' is everyday practice at many organizations. Guided by concepts such as self-management, holacracy, and a variety of agile concepts, responsibilities are distributed throughout the entire organization. Management control, however, is often still organized in a strictly hierarchical way, which does not suit these new practices and needs to be changed with the help of smart technology.

✓ **Invest in different competencies in the finance function**

The work of administrators and controllers (i.e. the data collectors) is becoming more and more automated so there is a growing need for data specialists who are able to build forecasting models that will enable teams throughout the organization to work autonomously. This type of do-it-yourself environment requires fewer and fewer business controllers.

✓ **Start learning instead of checking in the PDCA cycle**

Every organization needs good feedback mechanisms to be able to adapt to any rapid development. The traditional PDCA cycle could be such a feedback mechanism, provided the C of *check* is interpreted correctly. It is more about *learning* rather than *checking*. This is the reason that its inventor, Deming, always talked about the PDSA cycle, in which the S stands for *study*

## 8.2 Connect the dots in the data

*Nearly all areas of society are becoming increasingly specialized, in part because of a wave of technological innovation. This is fine, in itself, provided that generalists are able to seamlessly connect specialist insights. This 'connecting tissue' is necessary to prevent specialists from working in isolation, staying in their own bubble, as it were, without actually contributing to the shared strategic goal.*

*This also applies to data-related projects. Specialist expertise is often needed to make a difference in a particular domain. But only if there is sufficient cohesion between all organizational parts (and, where necessary, also with parties within an ecosystem) can these projects actually contribute to the strategy. CFOs are the holistic conscience and should supervise this process.*

Endocrinology, nephrology, haematology, vascular surgery, traumatology, oncological surgery, gastrointestinal surgery, paediatric haematologists, eye specialists, lung oncologists, phlebologists, dermatologists, electrocardiologists, and reproductive endocrinology and infertility specialists. These are some of a growing number of specializations in the healthcare sector, courtesy of Marcel Levi, CEO of University College London Hospitals, who wrote a piece about it on the Dutch healthcare website 'Huisarts & Wetenschap'.[100] In the article, he particularly calls on the care sector to ensure proper connection between all these specialists. He points out that things are not going as they should in this respect, with patients who have more than one disease 'travelling through the hospital like nomads, from specialist to specialist, with all the communication problems that entails'. Several studies prove

Levi right. It is precisely in patients being transferred from one healthcare specialist to the next that things go wrong; holistic approaches are hard to find, partly due to information systems that cannot handle the proper transfer of such information.[101]

## Holistic approach

This book is not about the care sector. It is about the role of CFOs in an era in which decisions are increasingly made on the basis of data. Nevertheless, the excursion into care is relevant to understand why a holistic approach is also essential with regard to the Decision Oriented Organization.

After all, similar specialization – and the associated struggle for a successful holistic approach – can be seen within the realm of data and data analysis. There are specialists who, for example, focus on social media, and, within that group of specialists, others who then specialize in, for instance, sentiment analysis or customer journeys. There are also those who optimize the supply chain through the smart use of data. There are business intelligence specialists who search through data to uncover the best insights, or process mining analysts who work with data to make certain activities even more efficient. Then there are the specialists who know everything there is to know about dynamic pricing – all based on data, of course – as well as subspecializations with unclear distinctions between them such as data engineer, data scientist, and data analyst.

Just as a holistic approach is needed in healthcare to provide patients with the best treatment and experience, so it is also necessary to take a holistic approach to the use of all kinds of techniques and concepts that contribute to a Decision Oriented Organization.

We are convinced that CFOs are uniquely able to take on this holistic role and are capable of 'connecting the dots'. If they do, their organization will truly become one that is decision-oriented and therefore prepared for any future change. CFOs have an excellent starting position in this area as well. In their traditional role, for decades, they have worked very closely with almost all internal disciplines and have been trained to oversee the whole. They are, therefore, by experience already in the position of 'synthesizer'. Moreover, if McKinsey's analysis[102] is to be believed, CFOs are actively developing their skills in this area: 'The gamut of roles that reported to the CFO role has dramatically increased. On average, approximately six discrete roles are reporting to the CFO today. Those roles range from procurement to investor relations, which, in some companies, tend to be very finance-specific. Two years ago, that average was around four.'

**CFOs applying the glue**
This development is further accelerated by the digital transformation that plays a major role within almost every organization. In this transformation, CFOs are not power hungry and wanting to pull all the strings, but they are in a position to apply the proverbial glue to connect functions, departments, and project teams.

Which is nice, but it is not enough.

End-to-end thinking has to become the new normal in many IT projects. The term 'end to end' is used in all kinds of publications, and it is a very simple concept. The 'old normal' meant processes were carried out in functional departments such as purchasing, logistics, and marketing. This is very different in end-to-end processes, which run diagonally across such departments. In a digital environment, this also means that systems and applications are interlinked in order to make these processes end to end. Modern ERP systems also explicitly facilitate the increased connectivity.

In many projects, however, end-to-end thinking is still a long way off, even though it is a prerequisite for success. It is great when an organization has access to good data and corresponding algorithms, but this will only deliver value when implemented in the relevant organizational processes. And that can only be achieved with a consistent end-to-end vision.

### Implementing analytics

Take, for example, the optimization of public transport in a city. Data scientists looking at data from various sources, and with or without using advanced AI, will undoubtedly be able to uncover possibilities to improve the routing schedule of bus operators to better respond to the needs of passengers. For example, they could likely develop a fantastically dynamic transport schedule that is in lockstep with real-time predictions about passenger travel demand and traffic congestion. However, the fact that such an analysis would provide clever insights, in itself, carries no value.

Such insights will not lead to value unless they are implemented seamlessly by the organization's departments or other parties involved. For example, there would need to be a link with the travel information systems and the insights should serve as input for HR departments to organize the scheduling of drivers. With respect to equipment management, the consequences are also significant, for example, when scheduling maintenance or charging electric buses.

Thus, the real benefits of data and data analysis cannot be harvested until organizations begin working with an end-to-end vision. This applies to virtually every sector and often extends beyond individual organizations. Take supermarkets: optimizing stocking the shelves and/or the pricing of products on those shelves not only requires seamless links between the systems involved within a supermarket group itself, but also with the suppliers and logistics parties involved. An end-to-end approach in this case means establishing a connection between cash register systems, suppliers' systems, and those of logistics. And, in the future, perhaps would require a link with your fridge at home.

And so, CFOs should demolish any walls that still exist between departments and organizations and take charge of matters such as data definitions so that connections run smoothly and optimally.

## Platforms

The emergence of platforms – i.e. network orchestrators – is perhaps the best proof that end-to-end thinking is needed to achieve success. End to end is actually the name of the game for *all* platform companies. After all, they exist by virtue of excelling in end-to-end thinking; success means they arrange connections between parties and do so better, faster, and cheaper than others. Returning to the metaphor of the rainforest and the plantation, companies like Uber and Airbnb are structuring their environment – a rainforest – by using smart systems. They adopt fully automated decision-making on the basis of advanced algorithms.

## Organization

The end-to-end thinking about data is not a plea for highly centrally managed data initiatives with CFOs in charge, because that would put a brake on all of the valuable decentralized initiatives. The most appropriate model would be a hybrid one, as shown in figure 8.2.[103] The following chapter describes the design principles in more detail.

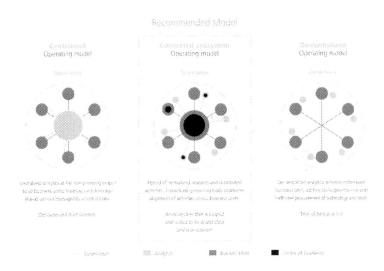

Figure 8.2 The recommended operating model

## Core messages to CFOs:

✓ **Be the holistic conscience for an organization when it comes to data**

Data-driven work methods require smooth connections between departments within organizations and/or organizations within the same ecosystem. CFOs could stimulate this by being the ones to forge the connections and take down the walls.

✓ **Develop a hybrid operating model for analytics**

Central analytics management will contribute to the much-needed holistic thinking within organizations. However, decentralized models would stimulate bottom up innovation. The challenge, thus, is to develop a hybrid model in which both are combined as much as possible.

# PART 3
# DOING IS THE BEST KIND OF THINKING

On how to start transforming into a Decision
Oriented Organization

# Chapter 9  Design principles for building a Decision Oriented Organization

## Plotting decisions on speed and impact

*There is really no doubt about a new reality emerging in business, one in which competition, more than ever, is settled through excellence in decision-making. In Chapters 6,7, and 8 of this book, we shared insights on what CFOs can do to prepare their organization and how they can transform their businesses into decision-oriented organizations that will be successful in this new reality. But this also calls for a tailor-made approach since every organization and/or department has its specific characteristics. In this chapter we give some guidance on design principles that are connected to the specific challenges of an organization, based on a simple model that may stimulate the right type of debate on the priorities to be set.*

One of the most famous quirky one-liners by legendary Dutch football player and coach, Johan Cruijff, reads: 'You won't see it until you realize it' (*Je gaat het pas zien als je het doorhebt*). This also applies to Decision Oriented Organizations. Anyone who realizes that a different way of making decisions is emerging will also realize suddenly that it is necessary to look at organizations from a completely different perspective. This is only the beginning though. The next issue would be how to design an organization that is prepared for this new reality. To start, we need to analyse what a decision actually is. Every decision has at least two dimensions.

First, there is the speed at which decisions are made (or need to be made). In some cases, a decision can take weeks or even months (e.g. in the case of research into a new product or acquisition), while in other cases decisions must be made instantly (e.g. the automatic purchase of advertising space on the Internet).

The second characteristic of decisions is their impact. Agreed, decisions are all of a certain importance – otherwise there would be no need for them – but what is at stake varies from case to case. A decision about where to purchase office supplies will, at least in most cases, have less of an impact than one about whether or not to invest in highly strategic new projects.[104]

Plotting those two characteristics along two axes creates a simple matrix with four types of decisions as is shown in table 9.1, using the Formula 1 analogy.

|  | Low Speed | High Speed |
|---|---|---|
| High Impact | Selection of engine partner | Pit stop timing |
| Low Impact | Agreement on sponsor deal | Continuous changes in engine setup |

Table 9.1 Decision types

The High Impact type of decision is at the top right of the matrix. Formula 1 teams make rapid decisions about the best pit stop strategy based on how the race is going. The timing of pit stops is particularly important in races where overtaking is difficult. There are multiple examples of races where winning had depended on precisely that decision. Decisions with this level of impact also determine corporate success or failure.

At the top left of the matrix, we find decisions that also have a very high impact but do not need to be made within an instant. There is often time for proper analysis and consideration. An example of this is the choice of engine supplier, an agreement that is often entered into for several years. Red Bull Racing, for example, switched their engine supplier in 2018 from Renault to Honda – a much debated decision with much at stake and which involved thorough preparatory research.

At the bottom right, there are decisions of a slightly lower level of importance but that do need to be made very quickly. In the racing world, continuously changing the setup of the engine is an example of such decisions. Driver and team work together to tweak the setup of the engine during a race so that they are able to respond directly to things like changing temperatures, lap times of competitors, or gearbox malfunctions. Although such an operational perspective' is important, small mistakes often are not immediately fatal.

Finally, at the bottom left are the decisions with relatively little at stake and that require no immediate action. In the world of Formula 1, decisions about sponsorship fall in this category. Of course, it is important for teams to negotiate good sponsorship contracts if only because of the high costs involved in running a top team, but for the team's performance it probably makes little difference whether they are sponsored by an insurance company or one that sells soft drinks.

## Preconditions for decision-making processes

Using this simple model, leaders can plot the dynamics of their organization or of specific processes or units. In itself, this does not provide any operational perspective, but that changes as soon as design principles are linked to the various types of decisions.

Four different design principles can be defined. Two of them are related to the speed of decision-making:

*Autonomy.* If rapid decision-making is needed, it is often not feasible to have those decisions made via a hierarchical process starting at the top. Such situations require an organizational form in which teams and/or individual professionals have a large amount of autonomy.

*Level of automation.* Computers are often faster at understanding data and calculating scenarios, so rapid decisions in many cases call for a relatively high level of automation. Especially those where an infinite number of options are unfathomable for human decision-makers.

The other two are related to impact:
*Investment.* Organizations should invest in high-impact projects. CFOs know how to both prioritize capital expenditure for such projects and save costs as much as possible on less important matters. This also applies to decision-making pro-

cesses; if the impact is high, this justifies large investment in resources that would improve those processes.

*Reliability.* Every decision requires reliable data as well as logic (or algorithms). But when the impact of a project is likely to be high, nothing should go wrong in the related decision-making process. Such high-impact decisions, therefore, require a great deal of attention paid to reliability.

These four can also be represented in the following matrix (table 9.2):

|  | Low Speed | High Speed |
|---|---|---|
| High Impact | Autonomy low | Autonomy high |
|  | Level of automation low | Level of automation high |
|  | Investment high | Investment high |
|  | Reliability high | Reliability high |
| Low Impact | Autonomy low | Autonomy high |
|  | Level of automation low | Level of automation high |
|  | Investment low | Investment low |
|  | Reliability low | Reliability low |

Table 9.2 Organizational design principles related to decision types

Now the matrix suddenly looks eloquent. It really becomes a mirror to reflect whether the organization is indeed setting the right priorities. It can be used to answer many different questions such as: Is money being spent on the things that matter most? Is there sufficient autonomy in the organization to enable rapid decision-making? What is the quality of the data on which impactful decisions are made?

These questions lead to the right debate on what would be needed for good decision-making processes.

Organizations using the model as their starting point when making decisions will avoid the risks that are related to following the newest trend in technology or management, since the choices that present themselves flow from the model. Having a large degree of self-management is not an end in itself, but it is necessary for making certain types of decisions. And this is also true with respect to investments in artificial intelligence, which only make sense in certain cases.

More generally speaking, there are three things relevant to excellence in decision-making: the right data; the right decision rules based on that data; and the actual implementation and adherence to the decision-making process. This third point requires perseverance; many professionals tend to revert back to old models, trusting Excel sheets more than smart algorithms.

## CFO profiles

CFOs are typically suited to shape the Decision Oriented Organization (see the related arguments in Chapter 1). For the various types of decisions, this implies the need for different roles. When issuing their advice on the interpretation of the finance function, we could use a Deloitte model in which CFOs have four faces. These four faces – whether or not combined in one person – can be seamlessly linked to the model.

|  | Low Speed | High Speed |
|---|---|---|
| High Impact | CFO: strategist | CFO: catalyst |
| Low Impact | CFO: steward | CFO: operator |

Table 9.2 Decision types and the face of the CFO

Deloitte describes these roles as follows:

### Catalyst
– *CFOs can stimulate and drive the timely execution of change in the finance function or the enterprise. Using the power of their purse strings, they can selectively drive business improvement initiatives such as improved enterprise cost reduction, procurement, pricing execution, and other process improvements and innovations that add value to the company.*

### Strategist
– *CFOs take a seat at the strategy planning table and help influence the future direction of the company. They are vital in providing financial leadership and aligning business and finance strategy to grow the business. In addition to M&A and capital market financing strategies, they can play an integral role in supporting other long-term investments of the company.*

### Steward
– *CFOs work to protect the vital assets of the company, ensure compliance with financial regulations, close the books correctly, and communicate value and risk issues to investors and boards.*

### *Operator*
– *CFOs have to operate an efficient and effective finance organization providing a variety of services to the business such as financial planning and analysis, treasury, tax, and other finance operations.*

Organizations deserve a combination of these roles that would fit any specific challenge. In many cases, the catalyst role will be crucial in building a Decision Oriented Organization as this will involve radical change. The next chapter discusses this change in more detail.

# Chapter 10  Change: Where to begin?

Action speaks louder than words

*The first sentence of this book claims that we're approaching a historic moment in Formula 1. The moment in which machines are outperforming human drivers. The chapters that followed showed that such a historic moment is looming for business as well. Data-driven decisions are becoming the norm, and companies need to transform themselves into Decision Oriented Organizations.*

*We also concluded that many changes are needed.*

*Change rarely happens by itself. It needs an incentive. The question in this case is where such an incentive would come from.*

*The simplest answer would be the customer. Customers look for convenience, speed, and usefulness of new data applications and expect organizations to provide them. The organizations that fail to do so will soon be out of business. And, yet, this is only half the story. Because responding only to the changing wishes of customers would risk making only incremental innovations – which would be a gross misunderstanding of what is really going on.*

*Fundamental change needs to come from the realization that data really will fuel every activity and that success means outperforming the competition in obtaining a firmer grip on the future, which in turn mainly relates to the way the data is used.*

*It is about the difference between 'doing things differently' and 'doing different things' – yet another thing that is well and truly understood in the world of Formula 1 racing.*

In the 1990s, Unilever Vlees Groep were in severe financial trouble and their management operations were not in order. Top executive Tex Gunning came up with an unorthodox idea. He took all the staff on what they at first thought was a work outing to the Efteling amusement park but, in actual fact, was a trip to a Unilever factory, where he showed them 3,700 pallets of rejected goods that were piled up from floor to ceiling. Total value: around € 4 million. There were labels indicating what food products were in which crates, showing the reason why they could not be sold and what the financial losses amounted to. Subsequently, as the staff looked on, Gunning had forklift trucks take the crates and dump them outside in a huge pit. The purpose of the operation was to shock employees into realizing that there were a number of things fundamentally wrong at the company.

It was a powerful way of showing them that something needed to change. As they say in management: showing them the burning platform.[105] The idea behind his thinking was that if an entire organization is aware that there is an acute crisis, this forms an excellent basis for organizational change.

The previous chapters describe the need for change on many fronts. The success of such change partly depends on technology and partly – for the largest part – the human element. By confronting them with the 3,700 pallets of rejected goods, Gunning motivated his employees and propelled them into action. Within the context of the subject of this book, however, other things are required. Because often there is no burning platform.

## Preventing analysis paralysis

The risk of analysis paralysis looms around the theme of this book. The idea of a Decision Oriented Organization can be explored and discussed ad infinitum and all the while, nothing will happen. Those wanting to be absolutely certain about covering all perspectives in the analysis will remain stuck in this phase of deliberation. If we had followed such an approach for this book, there would be no book today – or ever. In the words of Voltaire: perfect is the enemy of good.

And then there is the fact that thinking and analysing are held in high regard, in the world of finance as elsewhere. Thinking is prestigious, which is one of the reasons why we like to go to events where we can hear important people from all corners of society speak. They inspire us and, afterwards, we can boast about what we have learned. This results in beautiful analyses and well-aimed one-liners about the necessary change – but not necessarily to action.

## Action mode

The question then is how to avoid this paralysis. How can we get from thinking to doing.

Here too the analogy with Formula 1 is illustrative:
In November 2019, Dutch racing driver Max Verstappen drove his car to victory after a spectacular race full of incidents on the Brazilian circuit, Interlagos. After the race, during the award ceremony, Max Horner, leader of the Red Bull Racing team (Verstappen's team), decided to send Hannah Schmitz to the podium with Verstappen to break out the champagne. The Dutch television commentator demeaningly referred to her as 'the data girl'.[106] This data girl, it bears stressing, has a Master's degree from the prestigious University of Oxford as well as 10 years of experience as a racing strategist.

### Devilish dilemma

Later, Horner explained to the press why he had put his senior strategic officer in the spotlight. Schmitz had played a crucial role in Verstappen's victory by recommending he change his tyres one more time a few laps before the finish. At that moment, the safety car was on the track because two Ferraris had collided. A pit stop for fresh and faster tyres would cost relatively little time because the other cars were following the safety car at low speed. On the other hand, the pit stop would mean that Verstappen would be handing the lead to Mercedes driver Lewis Hamilton. This was risky, as he would then have to try and take back the lead from the six-time world champion.

Schmitz was faced with a near-impossible choice – with only a few seconds to decide. A high-impact, high-speed decision. As a strategist, however, she was prepared for just such a situation. In preparing for a race, hundreds of scenarios are calculated; using real time data from, among other things, hundreds of sensors on the car, she was able to predict which choice was the most likely to lead to victory.

The case illustrates the incentive for data-driven decisions in Formula 1 – the only thing that counts is winning and data is a sound basis on which decisions are made. The commentator's somewhat sneering remark about her being the 'data girl' is not insignificant in this respect. Certain conventions and routines, apparently, are still front of mind among members of the older generation who are not yet aware of the dawn of a new age.

Such an incentive to win is not used very often in organizations to make them more data driven.

Many companies make only half-hearted attempts at change because they fail to understand the vitally important role of excellence in decision-making – data-driven or otherwise. To get to the bottom of this, here we distinguish between 'doing things differently' and 'doing different things'.

## Doing things differently

Fortunately, many companies take their customers' wishes very seriously. One of those wishes concerns smooth digital services, in all areas of life, which can only be achieved if data processes are up to speed, as described in previous chapters.

This type of customer focus can be very successful, as numerous companies are showing. In an international context, Amazon is one of the trendsetters, with behind the scenes a highly data-driven approach. A good example of the aim to anticipate customer wishes is Amazon submitting their application, a few years ago, for a patent titled Anticipatory Shipments.[107] In other words, Amazon intends to ship your parcels before you have even ordered them!

Anticipating the desires of customers, however, is no guarantee for building a successfully data-driven organization. It can also lead to partial solutions: applications that are being modernized on the front end while things are left the way they are behind the scenes. In other words, operations are updated only for the sake of appearances.

And there is yet another risk. Customers, generally speaking, lack the imagination to define what it is that they would really want. When asked about the development of his model T Ford, Henry Ford is claimed to have said:, 'if I had asked people what they really wanted, they would have said "a faster horse"'. The theory being that people cannot imagine the thing they do not know. This also applies to the use of data. For example, in the pre-data era, Max Verstappen could not have imagined data making the difference and delivering his win – that data specialists would be able to work out how to gain the advantage, using data to create hundreds of racing scenarios so that winning decisions could be made in a split second.

In short, building a data-driven organization by following the wishes of consumers will only lead to doing the same things as before, yet differently. While *doing different things* is what is truly needed.

### Doing different things

French author Marcel Proust once wrote about exploration, 'the true voyage of discovery is not about looking for new horizons, but about having new eyes'.

He hit the proverbial nail on the head for those intending to make the change towards a Decision-Oriented Organization.

This begins with embracing a totally different way of decision-making, one in which success is increasingly determined by being able to make slightly better-informed decisions than those made by the competition. Just like 'data girl' Hannah Schmitz did in a split second during the Brazilian Grand Prix, beating her team's competitors. This was not a question of doing things differently, but of doing different things.

CFOs must have the imagination to see that difference with crystal clarity and act accordingly. In practical terms, over the past decades CFOs emerged as being very valuable in improving the performance of their organizations – by doing things differently. They evolved from bean counters to strategic sparring partners. These days, they also need an innovative vision on how to be more successful with the best decisions based on the best data. And to then let that vision permeate through their organization.

CFOs are the ones with the expertise, position, and experience to build that new reality, as we argued earlier. This is a good thing but now it is time for the next step: they must also be the ones to set the wheels in motion.

**But how?**

There is no fixed recipe for success. In reality, such transformations almost always involve *wicked problems*.[108] These are problems with conflicting and changing conditions and a multitude of relationships between whichever things or people involved. One of the characteristics of *wicked problems* is that there are no right or wrong solutions. Only those that are better or worse. It is precisely for this reason that this book does not contain a manual on how to successfully complete the transformation. However, it does formulate three general lessons based on practical experiences and scientific insights: 1) CFOs should bring the overarching objective – the purpose – to life; 2) CFOs should synthesize sources of information and 3) CFOs should use shocks to really get things in motion.

Let's look in more detail.

### 1. Change requires bringing the purpose of a Decision Oriented Organization to life

For people to become truly motivated into 'doing other things', they must have a firm notion of the need for such a change, defined here as the *purpose*. In practice, this is often more difficult than first envisaged. The difficulty is not in formulating a number of proper principles during a few strategic management sessions, but rather in really bringing them into focus and ensuring that other people in the organization will be able to use those principles when setting priorities and implementing choices. Anyone who assumes that such vital changes can be made in broad strokes is bound to become extremely disappointed.

An example of what is needed: At the beginning of this century, waste processing company Van Gansewinkel left little to the imagination when formulating its strategic objective (i.e. its purpose). Their simple and often-praised branding phrase 'Waste no more' (*Afval bestaat niet*) clarified to everyone inside and outside the organization that the company saw waste, first and foremost, as yet another material and a source of energy. At the time, this was a powerful message that could not be misunderstood by personnel and external parties. In order for it to be more than a marketing slogan – about which there was no doubt in Van Gansewinkel's case – processes (including decision-making) must be designed in such a way that the entire organization is able to contribute to the objective on each and every working day.

In the military, this is represented in the concept of the commander's intent. Every order given on the battlefield is clearly understood as part of that intent. The historical background of this concept is that all those in the field need to know what the military intentions are, so that if they become cut off from their battalion or superiors in the chaos and complexity of battle, they will still be able to make choices that contribute to the intended objective. In the words of former general Tom Kolditz, 'You can lose the ability to execute the original plan, but you never lose the responsibility of executing the intent'.[109] The 'why' is always crystal clear and is even literally given in the order.

Back to the transformation towards becoming a decision-oriented organization. Here, too, people 'in the field' first need to know why they are doing what they are doing – why they are working towards becoming a Decision Oriented Organization – and, secondly, be able to translate this into what it means for each individual.

The first is already difficult enough and calls for CFOs, in their role as architect of the Decision Oriented Organization, to develop into inspired storytellers (also see Chapter 1). The second – translating it to the organization – is possibly even more challenging.

This is precisely where our model for analysing the types of decisions comes into play. This model helps not only in obtaining a clear view of the impact and speed of decision; as we have seen in Chapter 9, this model also helps in translating this view into design principles (Autonomy, Level of Automation, Investment, Reliability).

*2. Start synthesizing current initiatives*
In earlier chapters, we show that building a Decision Oriented Organization is a multi-headed dragon. Many organizations currently have multiple initiatives aimed at better use of data for decisions. Information sources are mushrooming as a consequence of further digitization of processes: nearly everything is measurable and there are nearly endless possibilities to generate insights.

A famous old quote, in this context, is from Edward O. Wilson: 'We're drowning in data and starving for wisdom.' Less well-known is the remainder of the original quote, which is longer and continues as follows: 'The world henceforth will be run by synthesizers, people able to put together the right information at the right time, think critically about it, and make important choices wisely.'

This sentence perfectly summarizes the role of CFOs and their teams in this work. Data-driven work methods require smooth connections between departments within organizations and/or organizations within the same ecosystem. CFOs could stimulate this by being the ones to forge the connections and take down the walls.

*3. Change requires administering small shocks*
It more or less goes without saying that initiating change processes calls for training sessions and workshops; these are instruments that can contribute to the desired change. But their effect should not be overestimated and, moreover, change managers are increasingly realizing that effective change can also or especially be achieved via the opposite route.

The point of training courses is that of informing people about why change is necessary, in the hope that they will put that change into practice. But suppose this would be the other way around, i.e. that changes would simply be implemented, on a small scale or even just in pilot projects. Figuratively speaking, 'shocking' people into changing. This would likely lead to questions and more detailed discussions about the need for change, and thus provide a better breeding ground for structural change.

Such shocks can therefore have a much greater effect than any large-scale training programme. Shocks can be anything; e.g. changing the tasks of a department overnight, developing a new application without explaining the reason for its implementation, or changing the interior or accommodation of a certain department without prior notice. Such structural changes can be exactly what is needed to initiate cultural change – the most difficult aspect of any such transformation – and tempt those on the floor to participate or even take control themselves.

These types of opportunities are readily available to be used for the transformation into a Decision Oriented Organization. After all, developing the digital applications for this purpose, possibly based on artificial intelligence, is often a matter of experimenting, adjusting, and/or starting over. The most effective strategy can be to 'just do' and gradually discover the way to go.

In their analysis in the *Harvard Business Review*,[110] Walker and Soule rightly state that such transformation involves starting a movement and they underline the importance of the above. It is mainly about *demonstrating* change instead of passionately arguing in favour of it. The authors write: 'leaders too often fall into the trap of declaring the culture shifts they hope to see. Instead, they need to spotlight *examples of actions* they hope to see more of within the culture.'

Now, that's the challenge for CFOs. Be the change that you want to see.

# PART 4
# DECISION TIME

On why CFOs shouldn't wait until tomorrow

# Chapter 11   Timing the wave

*Finally, there is the important yet often neglected question of the timing of the change described in the previous chapters. Generally speaking, timing is one of the most difficult strategic issues in innovation. Investing in innovation too early often causes large capital losses. The returns on such projects are often insufficient, technology is still too immature, or the market is not yet ready for it. Starting investments too late, however, risks missing the boat. Catching up with competitors often is very expensive and sometimes requires the procurement of companies that did innovate on time. Like surfing the waves, proper timing is the only way to succeed.*

*The question, therefore, is whether now would be the right time for CFOs to focus fully on building Decision Oriented Organizations. The short answer is yes. The longer – substantiated – answer is elaborated on the following pages.*

When the Internet first emerged during 1990s, nobody wanted to miss out and companies invested large amounts of money in websites and e-commerce ventures. Usually they did not have a real, coherent vision of the meaning or future importance of the Internet. Many of the original investments evaporated when the initial hype gave way to realism. These first Internet companies turned out to be unable to live up to the unrealistically high ratings and, once the house of cards collapsed, owners discovered their wealth to exist mainly on paper. But meanwhile, development of the Internet did continue and, between 2000 and 2010, many companies started to work consistently on their digital strategy. Trial and error showed them the true meaning of the Internet.

In the decade that followed, smartphones conquered the world and, also on other fronts, there was talk of what actually constituted a refinement of Internet techniques. In management literature in the United States, the term SMAC[111] emerged to describe certain trends (i.e. Social, Mobile, Analytics, and Cloud). At the same time, the 'AI winter'[112] had come to an end, and AI applications are emerging in society. This combination of rapidly emerging techniques and concepts creates a perfect storm in the technology landscape. Once again, similar to the rise of the Internet, many companies are freeing up money and resources for any number of projects, and again, disappointment is rising when investments fail to live up to expectation. The hype around Artificial Intelligence has also met with opposition in recent years, as experts critically question the number of implemented useful applications. But, below the surface, developments continue at an unprecedented pace.

This brief historical look offers a valuable lesson about whether now is the time to put all the efforts into building Decision Oriented Organizations.

This time it is not about understanding what the Internet means in a strategic sense, but about understanding that, from now on, competition will be won by whoever builds the best information processing machine to make the best decisions and being the most successful at anticipating the future. In other words: whoever builds the best Decision Oriented Organization.

Such an organization must be able to excel in processing information from both inside and outside the organization. In this respect, it is important to be aware of the pattern of information development. In the words of futurologist Stewart Brand (1984), 'information wants to be free'. Free as in 'without costs'. His simple mantra took on a life of its own in the years that followed and he was regularly misinterpreted. In *Fortune Magazine*,[113] Brand once again pointed to what, at the time, had been the essence of his remark: 'My original point is that because the technology keeps moving, it keeps the tension alive between free and expensive, so it never stabilises. In a sense, this rewards the innovative and punishes those who can't innovate or change rapidly.'

Information is nevertheless certainly becoming more cost-free. Even though there is much – well-deserved – attention on privacy, it is also clear that data is increasingly publicly available. Bearing in mind the harsh laws of thermodynamics, there seems to be maximum entropy (disorder) in the information landscape. The genie is out of the bottle, with information finding its own way.

Everybody knows that eggs cannot be unscrambled. And so, there is no other option than to face the new challenge of competing on who makes the best decisions based on the best information. There is no more time to waste. Around the year 2000, companies like Google and Amazon were the new kids on the block, signs that profound change was imminent. They seized the opportunities of digitization in the optimal way.

And then there's one more historic and unanticipated thing: COVID-19.

At turbocharged speed, the pandemic has taught us many things. In all honesty, when it comes to business, nobody knew what to do when lockdowns of whole sectors started, but some responded better than others. Remember what we said about this in the introduction?

If you're in control you can go faster.

During the COVID-19 crisis it soon became crystal clear that swift availability and quality of data and the relevant tools and capabilities were key for a proper response. Whether you want to assess the financial health and liquidity of a company, develop scenarios on how to respond to the situation at hand and how to recover from it, or ensure that all finance operations continue to run, having a Decision Oriented Organization is key. Many companies still had to extract information from multiple accounting and reporting systems while the crisis unfolded. Some had to perform manual data cleansing, manipulation and analysis in spreadsheets, and put everything into a PowerPoint presentation to make it digestible for the main decision makers.

They were frozen in apathy for some time while they didn't have the time in this sink or swim situation. This pandemic therefore once more proved that we need to shift from traditional two-dimensional spreadsheets towards thinking in endless dimensions of data. Leveraging advanced analytics and visualization technologies, they should be able to run complicated scenario analyses in almost real time and facilitate fact-based and informed decision-making about the best course of action.

And who knows, in an ideal world, Decision Oriented Organizations might be able to predict the next disaster before it strikes.

Wouldn't that be fantastic?

# NOTES

## Introduction
1. https://www.spiegel.de/plus/sebastian-vettel-wuenscht-sich-fuer-seinen-ferrari-ein-schaltgetriebe-a-00000000-0002-0001-0000-000163724175

## Chapter 1
2. https://www.mckinsey.com/business-functions/strategy-and-corporate-finance/our-insights/the-new-cfo-mandate-prioritize-transform-repeat
3. *The Reckoning, Financial Accountability and the Rise and Fall of Nations*, Jacob Soll (2013) Basic Books, New York City, NY
4. https://callingbullshit.org/syllabus.html#Ecology
5. https://hbr.org/2013/07/why-cant-a-cio-be-more-like-a-CFO?

## Chapter 2
6. https://twitter.com/bchesky/status/421856850384932864
7. https://www.cbs.nl/nl-nl/nieuws/2019/32/nieuw-record-aantal-snelgroeiende-bedrijven
8. https://www.ing.com/Newsroom/All-news/Being-open-is-the-way-Ralph-Hamers.htm
9. https://www.wired.co.uk/article/rotterdam-port-ships-automation
10. https://www2.deloitte.com/us/en/pages/finance/articles/cfo-insights-digital-age-business-model-innovation-value.html
11. https://www2.deloitte.com/content/dam/Deloitte/nl/Documents/humancapital/deloitte-nl-hc-reshaping-work-conference.pdf
12. https://www.wsj.com/articles/peter-thiel-competition-is-for-losers-1410535536
13. http://platformed.info/unpacking-industry-4-0
14. That may sound like science fiction, but remember that Amazon has

already filed a patent under the name of 'Anticipatory Shipping'. In other words: sending a package before customers know they will be needing it.

**Chapter 3**

15. https://abovethecrowd.com/2015/01/30/ubers-new-bhag-uberpool
16. A salient detail in this context, is the fact that Blockbuster had once been able to acquire Netflix, but declined the offer. In the book *That Will Never Work*, Marc Randolph (co-founder of Netflix) describes a meeting at Blockbuster's headquarters in Dallas, where Netflix at the time was for sale for US$50 million. But Blockbuster's CEO would not even consider the idea. 'He seemed to see it as a great big joke.'
17. *Start with Why: How Great Leaders Inspire Everyone to Take Action*, Simon Sinek (2009) Penguin Group, New York City, NY
18. https://hbr.org/2015/12/what-is-disruptive-innovation
19. https://hbr.org/2011/01/the-big-idea-creating-shared-value

**Chapter 4**

20. This is when drivers find they are unable to overtake a competitor. They make a pit stop early to change their tyres in the hope that this will boost their timing so that they can get in front of their rival when it is his turn to head to the pits. It is an often-used catch-up strategy in modern-day Formula 1 racing.
21. https://netsotech.com/assets/documents/simplivity_caseStudy_redbull.pdf
22. https://www.autosport.com/f1/news/139582/f1-should-discuss-reducing-teams-data--brawn
23. https://www.accountant.nl/globalassets/accountant.nl/blad/2019-q1/acc_2019_q1_new_kid_zoekt_accountant.pdf
24. Having said that, there are limits to explaining. The more complex AI models become, the more difficult to explain their reasoning.
25. Book by management author Thomas Davenport
26. https://www.youtube.com/watch?time_continue=1&v=exHoDXqJXyQ
27. In fact, the McLaren team has even set up an advisory unit as a spin-off of the team's racing activities to help business better reap the value of data.
28. At the time of publication of this book (2020).

## Chapter 5

29. https://www.economist.com/leaders/2019/10/03/the-rise-of-the-financial-machines

30. *The Principles of Scientific Management*, Frederick Taylor (1911) Harper & Brothers, New York City, NY

31. https://www.economist.com/business/2015/03/05/the-quantified-serf

32. https://www.ft.com/content/6250e4ec-8e68-11e7-9084-d0c17942ba93

33. Chinese professor Feng Xiang wrote an analysis, intriguingly titled 'AI will spell the end of capitalism', in which he concluded "If the state controls the market instead of digital capitalism controlling the state, true communist aspirations will be achievable. And because AI increasingly enables the management of complex systems by processing massive amounts of data through intensive feedback loops, it presents, for the first time, a real alternative to the market signals that have long justified laissez-faire ideology – and all the ills that go with it." https://www.washingtonpost.com/news/theworldpost/wp/2018/05/03/end-of-capitalism/

## Chapter 6

34. https://video.foxnews.com/v/1678568321001

35. https://en.wikiquote.org/wiki/Ronald_Coase

36. https://www.oreilly.com/library/view/the-little-book/9781292148458/html/chapter-109.html

37. https://en.wikipedia.org/wiki/Lies,_damned_lies,_and_statistics

38. https://hbr.org/2012/08/make-the-case-for-better-qua

39. https://hbr.org/2016/09/bad-data-costs-the-u-s-3-trillion-per-year

40. https://www.gartner.com/smarterwithgartner/how-to-stop-data-quality-undermining-your-business

41. Incidentally, these studies can also be questioned in certain areas, with respect to the quality of the data on which these assumptions are based, but that is hardly the point here.

42. https://fd.nl/ondernemen/1277485/eindelijk-kan-intergamma-beginnen-aan-de-grote-verbouwing

43. Another, often heard version is that of 'What gets measured gets managed'. Neither expression can be attributed to Drucker with 100% certainty. Also see the discussion on https://athinkingperson.com/2012/12/02/who-said-what-gets-measured-gets-managed

44. *Infonomics, How to Monetize, Manage, and Measure Information as an Asset for Competitive Advantage*, Douglas B. Laney (2017), Routledge, London, UK

45. This is not always the case. In some organizations, the second line takes on too many responsibilities, creating an undesirable 'control tower'.
46. https://www.wired.com/2008/06/pb-theory
47. https://norvig.com/fact-check.html
48. https://www.labsix.org/physical-objects-that-fool-neural-nets
49. 'B.S.' stood for 'bullshit'
50. A test by Vice.com, reported here: https://www.vice.com/en_us/article/pa7dj9/flawed-algorithms-are-grading-millions-of-students-essays For more information about BABEL, see: http://lesperelman.com/writing-assessment-robo-grading/babel-generator
51. Growth in a time of debt, Carmen M. Reinhart and Kenneth S. Rogoff https://www.nber.org/papers/w15639
52. https://www.bloomberg.com/news/articles/2013-04-18/faq-reinhart-rogoff-and-the-excel-error-that-changed-history
53. https://www.sec.gov/news/press-release/2018-167
54. https://www.risk.net/asset-management/6119616/black-rock-shelves-unexplainable-ai-liquidity-models
55. *Big Data: A Revolution That Will Transform How We Live, Work, and Think*, Kenneth Cukier and Viktor Mayer-Schönberger (2013), Mariner Books, New York City, NY
56. https://competency.aicpa.org/media_resources/208455-reimagining-auditing-in-a-wired-world
57. A term introduced by Meredith Brousard in her book of the same name.
58. In addition, there is a related risk: if the parameters of the safety become known, fraudsters will adjust their methods accordingly, to avoid being caught. Gaming the system is a deeply ingrained human trait.
59. https://hbr.org/2019/09/dont-let-metrics-undermine-your-business
60. https://www.britannica.com/topic/broken-windows-theory
61. *Freakonomics, A Rogue Economist Explores the Hidden Side of Everything*, Steven D. Levitt and Stephen J. Dubner (2006), William Morrow, New York City, NY
62. For those interested, the Wikipedia page offers a wealth of explanations, examples and references. https://en.wikipedia.org/wiki/Simpsons_paradox
63. https://medium.com/s/story/what-algorithms-know-about-you-based-on-your-grocery-cart-b364e0ba545c

64. http://www.padsweb.rwth-aachen.de/wvdaalst
65. https://www.ft.com/content/386e57b2-52a9-11e8-b3ee-41e0209208ec
66. https://www.handelsblatt.com/today/companies/programmed-
    for-disaster-lidl-software-disaster-another-example-of-
    germanys-digital-failure/23582902.html
67. *Bridging Organization Design and Performance: Five Ways to Activate
    a Global Operation Model*, Gregory Kesler and Amy Kates (2015), Jos-
    sey-Bass, Hoboken, NJ
68. https://www.100pceffective.com/blog/exposing-the-hidden-factory
69. Statement made during a Future Decoded meeting, organized by Mi-
    crosoft in 2018.
70. https://sloanreview.mit.edu/article/do-you-need-a-data-dictator
71. What Are ERP Best-Practice Processes and When Should You Adopt
    Them?, 13 March 2019
72. Ross & Weill: 'Enterprise Architecture As Strategy: Creating a Foun-
    dation for Business Execution', 2006

**Chapter 7**
73. https://www.businessinsider.com/why-whatsapps-jan-koum-hates-
    being-called-an-entrepreneur-2014-2?IR=T
74. https://twitter.com/Verwaayen/status/1129016894164557824
75. https://www.zdnet.com/article/big-data-case-study-how-ups-is-
    using-analytics-to-improve-performance
76. With the growing use of data comes a growing concern about proper
    privacy. Properly dealing with these concerns is a vital topic in many
    sectors, especially in data-rich sectors such as insurance. In this book,
    we will not elaborate on this aspect.
77. https://twitter.com/jamet123/status/1116361262177239043
78. https://www.ft.com/content/4667b18c-5249-11ea-8841-482eed0038b1
79. https://www.economist.com/business/2020/03/24/the-coronavirus-
    crisis-thrusts-corporate-hr-chiefs-into-the-spotlight
80. http://fronesys.com/the-changing-flows-of-corporate-
    performance-information
81. http://newvantage.com/wp-content/uploads/2017/01/Big-Data-
    Executive-Survey-2017-Executive-Summary.pdf
82. https://www.zdnet.com/article/can-red-hat-save-ibm/
83. *The Psychopath Test: A Journey Through the Madness Industry*, Jon
    Ronson (2011), Tantor Media, Old Saybrook, CT
84. https://sites.insead.edu/facultyresearch/research/doc.cfm?did=50923

85. The Identification of Solution Ideas during Organizational Decision Making, Paul C. Nutt, *Management Science*, Vol. 39, No. 9 (September 1993)

86. https://medium.com/wise-insights/better-decision-making-600-better-results-with-this-trick-a3552f134494

87. https://www.zorgvisie.nl/blockchain-nu-ook-in-de-kraamzorg

88. *Thinking, Fast and Slow*, Daniel Kahneman (2013) Farrar, Straus and Giroux, New York City, NY

89. https://www.sciencedaily.com/releases/2008/04/080414145705.htm

90. Even more so. A lack of sleep is not cool at all. If you fail to get enough sleep, you will not be able to make the right decisions. This is the conclusion from a survey held among US entrepreneurs. The conclusion reads: "Far from being a sign of weakness, sleep can serve as an early-stage aid to effectively evaluate the myriad business opportunities to pursue. Sleeping at the right times, such as the night before ideation and evaluation tasks, will improve outcomes." https://hbr.org/2019/10/entrepreneurs-who-sleep-more-are-better-at-spotting-good-ideas

91. *Thinking, Fast and Slow*, Daniel Kahneman (2013) Farrar, Straus and Giroux, New York City, NY

92. Viktor Mayer Schönberger interviewed by Nart Wielaard.

**Chapter 8**

93. The term DevOps was coined by Patrick Debois, who organized the world's first 'devopsdays' conference.

94. Freely interpreted according to Marc Andreessen, see https://www.wsj.com/articles/SB10001424053111903480904576512250915629460

95. *The Rainforest: The secret to Building the Next Silicon Valley*, Victor Hwang and Greg Horowitt (2012) Regenwald, Los Altos Hills, CA

96. http://www.therainforestbook.com/pdf/White_paper_UC_Law.pdf

97. A governance model that has an organic, flat structure of 'circles'. The model became well known when it was applied by US company Zappos.

98. C-suite is the collective term for senior management executives, traditionally including CEO, COO, and CFO.

99. An elaborate historical analysis of how this went awry can be found at https://deming.org/uploads/paper/PDSA_History_Ron_Moen.pdf

100. https://www.henw.org/artikelen/de-eisen-van-moderne-gezondheidszorg

101. https://nos.nl/artikel/2250725-haperende-ict-in-de-zorg-verkeerde-medicatie-foute-beslissingen.html
102. https://www.mckinsey.com/business-functions/strategy-and-corporate-finance/our-insights/the-new-cfo-mandate-prioritize-transform-repeat
103. https://www2.deloitte.com/content/dam/Deloitte/nl/Documents/deloitte-analytics/deloitte-nl-data-analytics-point-of-view-becoming-an-insight-driven-organisation.pdf

### Chapter 9

104. In practice, impacts will have multiple dimensions, depending on the 'definition of success'. They may refer to profitability or quality of the workforce, market position, ecological footprint, or product quality. Users of the model can determine which combination of dimensions is involved, on a case-by-case basis.

### Chapter 10

105. All things considered, this term is often used in the wrong context. Dutch turnaround manager Klaas Wagenaar rightly says in his book *Fire* that the term had its origins in the disaster with the Piper Alpha drilling platform and that this disaster had no winners at all. This is in contrast to how the corporate world now often talks about burning platforms as a convenient way of setting a new course and becoming more successful.
106. https://autobahn.eu/artikel/55434/datameisje-van-red-bull-is-superstrateeg-die-race-voor-max-verstappen-won
107. https://www.sciencedirect.com/science/article/pii/S0305048317311283
108. The term has been popular in management literature in recent years, but was first coined by Horst Rittel and described in Rittel & Webber's paper 'Dilemmas in a General Theory of Planning' (1973).
109. Derived from *Made to Stick: Why Some Ideas Survive and Others Die*, Chip Heath and Dan Heath (2007) Random House, New York City, NY
110. https://hbr.org/2017/06/changing-company-culture-requires-a-movement-not-a-mandate

Chapter 11

111. https://searchcio.techtarget.com/definition/SMAC-social-mobile-analytics-and-cloud

112. As early as in the 1950s, artificial intelligence was already a theme in science. The initial interest was great but then died down, and it was not until decades later that it regained momentum.

113. https://fortune.com/2009/07/20/information-wants-to-be-free-and-expensive

# ABOUT THE AUTHORS

**Mohamed Bouker** (1978) is partner at Deloitte where he leads the Digital Finance practice for Deloitte Netherlands. He is passionate about new technologies and new ways of thinking. He advises local and international CFOs on their digital plans. With a background in ERP, Finance and data management, his core expertise lies in transforming financial processes with Robotics, Data Analytics, Best in Class Financial Systems and Cognitive Technology. He has also driven many Digital Finance strategies, financial process re-engineering initiatives and financial systems selection. He is a true believer in the power of data as the driver of businesses transformation.

**Frank Geelen** (1967) is the EMEA Lead Finance Transformation partner within Deloitte Consulting. He also leads the Deloitte CFO Program in The Netherlands and has a long-standing experience working with CFOs of the larger multinational companies to further improve their finance function. After a career in various finance management roles at Unilever and Royal Philips, Frank decided to move to consulting where he worked for IBM Consulting and PwC before joining Deloitte in 2011. He is passionate about the adoption of new (digital) technologies and enjoys working with client- and consulting teams discovering the 'art of the possible' and realizing the subsequent business benefits. He holds a master's degree in econometrics from the Erasmus University Rotterdam, a European master's degree in finance & control (RC) from the University of Amsterdam and an MBA from the Institute for Management Development (IMD) in Lausanne.

 **Nart Wielaard** (1970) was trained as a Certified Public Accountant. He now works as an independent business writer, public speaker and consultant. Wielaard is curious by nature and is fascinated by how digital technology impacts business and society as a whole. He helps clients turn complex topics into crisp and compelling stories and has authored multiple award-winning business books.

Printed in the United States
By Bookmasters